God's
Clowns

God's Clowns

*Messengers of
the Good News*

C. Welton Gaddy

1817

Harper & Row, Publishers, San Francisco

New York, Grand Rapids, Philadelphia, St. Louis
London, Singapore, Sydney, Tokyo, Toronto

FIRST EDITION

Library of Congress Cataloging-in-Publication Data

Gaddy, C. Welton.
    God's clowns : messengers of the good news / C. Welton Gaddy—
1st ed.
      p. cm.
      ISBN 0–06–252015–6
      1. Clowns—Religious aspects—Baptists.   2. Baptists—
Doctrines. I. Title.
      BV4235.C47G33   1990
      246'.7—dc20   89–45934
                                                CIP

---

90 91 92 93 94 HAD 10 9 8 7 6 5 4 3 2 1

This edition is printed on acid-free paper that meets the American National Standards Institute Z39.48 Standard.

Contents

Acknowledgments

In the spring of 1980 I preached a sermon entitled "Where Are the Clowns?" Members of Broadway Baptist Church in Forth Worth, Texas, a congregation in which I served as senior minister at that time, heard me attentively and responded positively. That marked the beginning of my interest in and enthusiasm for the subject of this volume.

Since that time I have shared various thoughts about the religious significance of the clown image with numerous university audiences, denominational meetings, and local churches. My audiences have been genuinely attracted to the metaphor and have frequently requested additional comments on the subject.

During my enjoyable tenure as senior minister to the university at Mercer University, with campuses in both Macon, Georgia, and Atlanta, Georgia, I researched a wide variety of materials on clowns, studied carefully pertinent biblical passages, and expanded my initial thoughts. I recorded my ideas and insights as brief notes, later lengthening them into paragraphs, and eventually developing them into essays. Strong support for my interests and efforts came from my close friend Raleigh Kirby Godsey, the president of Mercer University.

After I prepared an early draft of the manuscript, Floyd Thatcher read it and subsequently made me the beneficiary of his expertise as an editor and his support as a friend. I am sure that I would not have completed this project without Floyd's help.

Recently I became the pastor of the good people of the Highland Hills Baptist Church in Macon, Georgia. This caring congregation generously provided the time, space, and support that made possible the completion of this book.

Every word on the pages that follow has been typed numerous times by my patient and competent secretary, Betty Parsons, who unrelentingly believed in my work even when I questioned it.

Members of my immediate family—Judy, my wife, and John Paul and James Welton, our sons—have consistently encouraged my fascination with clowns, sensitively allowed me time for research and writing on the subject, and faithfully behaved as clowns.

The footnotes throughout the work give credit to various individuals for their insights. Undoubtedly I have also incorporated into my words the work of others unrecognized. Though I happily acknowledge my heavy dependence upon the thoughts of many persons, in no way do I make these people responsible for any of the limitations of these pages.

C. Welton Gaddy
Macon, Georgia

1.   Where Are the Clowns?

What fun is a circus without clowns? Or a parade without clowns? For that matter, what fun is life without clowns?

Clowns are those people who make us laugh and allow us to cry. Clowns captivate our attention, liberate our emotions, tickle our imagination, and enrich our vision. And it is clowns who reflect the pathos of desperate situations, tease us into festive celebration, cause us to grin at our humanity, and challenge us to entertain redemptive fantasies. We need clowns.

Some people enjoy being clowns almost as much as other people delight in seeing clowns. Life is enhanced inestimably by the presence of polka-dot-suited, flop-eared, frolicking clowns.

Personal Interest

My personal interest in clowns began as a child as I looked long and hard at the clown faces that stared back at me from slick circus posters. I studied clown clothes displayed in parades, and I was fascinated by clown antics in one-ring circuses.

I remember vividly the performers in those traveling circuses, and I watched the clowns with intensity and enjoyed their every movement. I was fascinated by all of the clowns: the fat ones, the thin ones, the short ones, those who stalked about on stilts, the jubilant jesters with their jumping dogs, and the agile riders perched atop their unicycles. And I liked the clowns who played musical instruments and those who looked too sad for songs.

I appreciated the antics of clowns long before I understood the importance of clowns. But then, on a red letter day in childhood I was given the opportunity to be a clown: a real clown with wide, red-painted triangular eyes and a huge smile. My excitement reached a fevered pitch as I put on tattered old clothes accented by glorious new ruffles, and worn-out, oversized shoes, and as I had makeup applied. Nothing up until then matched the exhilaration of anticipation, the excitement of the potential of clowning.

The parade that day was all that I had expected it to be. I was a part of the parade—as a clown—a running, walking, smiling, mocking, trick-playing clown. Effortlessly I reached out to the children and to the children in adults. People laughed and smiled as I pranced by.

What fun. What great fun! I was free: free to run, to skip, to dance, to joke, to jump, to laugh aloud with no inhibitions. After all, people expect such behavior from a clown. Even though the length of the parade route was too long for my short legs, it was too short for my soul. And by the time we clowns crossed the finish line, I was already looking forward to the next year and the opportunity to be a clown once again. It had all been so good. During those magic moments behind the painted face, inside the ragged clothes, I had become a person I wanted to be *all* the time: a sensitive, funny, spontaneous, generous, giving person. Yes. I like clowns.

My childhood fascination with clowns did not get "put away" with "childish things." Clown faces continue to capture my attention and evoke my appreciation. I am still a sucker for the circus jesters and parading entertainers—those heroes of hilarity.

Oh, sure, clowns feed on the imaginary in each of us, but quite honestly they often seem more real than many of the people around me. I prefer a clown anytime over an aluminum foil-covered float with plastic-faced, mannequin-like persons on top who mechanically wave their hands to the crowd but reveal nothing of their hearts. And I prefer a clown anytime over a kneeling elephant mastered by a trainer whose clothes glitter or a fashionably outfitted ringmaster who smiles only when the spotlight is on him. Clowns don't have to stay in line during parades or remain within rings under a big top. Clowns roam where they please, flirt with danger at ease, experiment with excitement, do as they will. I like that. I like those emissaries of exaggerated joy, the gourmets of goodwill. Bring on the clowns!

Not until adulthood was I introduced to rodeo clowns. In a dirt arena, spectators spot them right off—jaunting along on a mule, darting in and out of the spotlight, moving constantly among the stars in the opening parade prior to the posting of the colors. Throughout every performance these clowns seem to appear at strategic moments: during preparations for a calf-roping event or prior to the release of the bucking horses with their cowboy riders. And the clowns are in the arena constantly for the bareback riding of the Brahma bulls.

Spectators laugh heartily at the actions of this special breed of clown—taunting a pawing bull that is trying to goad a thrown rider or climbing quickly inside a rubber barrel that is about to be buffeted by the horns of a charging bull or leapfrogging over a snorting animal that has turned on the clown. In fact, sometimes rodeo buffs laugh so much at the clowns' antics that they fail to see how important those funny men and women are to the smooth running of the show.

But insiders know the value of the rodeo clowns, know that they are indispensable helpers for the cowboys. They draw the attention of enraged animals to themselves while dismounted riders scramble for safety. Rodeos could not go on safely or happily without such clowns. Could life?

Biblical Imagery

At some point in the past—"once below a time" as Frederick Buechner puts it[1]—a paragraph read or a sentence heard prompted me to begin exploring the relationship between clowns and Christians. Conditioned as I was by a strong conviction regarding biblical authority, I turned first to Scripture in pursuit of light on this intriguing subject.

I uncovered far more than I had anticipated. It was like what happens when you pull on a short thread from a swatch of woven fabric and then watch it unravel to a greater and greater length. My attention was first directed to an obvious passage in the writings of the Apostle Paul in which he makes a comment to the Christians at Corinth that suggests that the clown image is an apt characterization of a devoted Christian.

Paul was writing autobiography as well as theology when he said, "We are fools for Christ's sake" (1 Cor. 4:10). Obviously the important word in this statement is *fools.* How could Paul say such a thing about himself after what Jesus had said earlier, "Whoever says, 'you fool!' shall be liable to the hell of fire" (Matt. 5:22)?

The Greek word for *fool* in both verses is *moron,* and this immediately reminds us of our English word of derision that comes from this ancient root. It is interesting that the same word appears in verb form translated as "lost its taste," to describe what happens to salt (Christians) that is ruined (Matt. 5:13). We see from this that what Paul used positively, Jesus used negatively.

Unquestionably the older and primary meaning of *moron* was negative in nature. To call another person a fool was to dishonor that individual, to label that person empty-headed and frivolous.[2] And to label another person a fool indicated a distrust in his or her capacity for correct thought or action. Implied also was a lack of desire for fellowship. Similarly, in the parables of Jesus, the word *foolish* was used to describe those individuals who displayed a lack of common sense (Matt. 7:24–27, 25:1–13).

So we can't help but ask, How could Paul apparently have boasted about a statement of self-identity that most of his contemporaries would have taken as degrading? An answer to this question must involve a consideration of Paul's discussion of the gospel.

In Corinth the gospel was in trouble. The Jews had big problems with talk about a crucified Messiah. In their minds crucifixion was a curse, and the Messiah had to be a nonsuffering savior.

But the Greeks also had difficulty accepting the Christian message. In the first place they generally despised Jews, all of them. Consequently they couldn't see how divinely given salvation could possibly come by means of a Jew. And talk of crucifixion was considered a violation of proper etiquette. The retort of the world to the proclamation of the gospel was "foolishness" (1 Cor. 1:25) and "folly" (1 Cor. 1:18).

Make no mistake about it, the gospel of Jesus Christ was the problem, not the proclamation of that message. Paul wrote of "the folly of what we preach" (2 Cor. 1:21), not of the foolishness of preaching. As a matter of fact, preaching was popular. The people of ancient Corinth applauded oratory and appreciated polished rhetoric. It was the message, not the medium, that they couldn't accept.

Parallels exist in the present. Our society is much taken with persuasive speakers, even popular preachers. Most people appreciate the powerful dynamics of effective public speech. But the substance of the Christian gospel continues to give cause for concern. Jesus and his message actually fare little better today than they did in ancient Corinth. To speak of "living by dying" and "winning by losing," or of loving one's enemies and determining to wage peace in a warring world is to earn the retort of "Foolishness!" Perhaps the words are different: "You can't mean that!" "That is ridiculous." "Oh, come on, get serious!" The meaning, however, is the same.

Paul accepted the harsh judgments of his peers in Corinth, and then turned their words on them. In effect he said to them, "All right, you think the Christian gospel is foolish, but the foolishness of God is wiser than people" (1 Cor. 3:19). Paul's values were undergoing transformation. He had been mocked by the Athenians and charged with insanity by Festus. People could call him a fool if they so desired; he was proudly a fool for Christ.

In reality the redemptive actions of God do not make sense to this world. Given a choice, most people opt for retaliation rather than reconciliation. Few can truly understand exaltation by means of humiliation. Most of the world still looks at the cross as an unintelligible event, a foolish act, and views those who live by the way of the cross as foolish persons. Human reason recognizes no other interpretations.

Actually, we shouldn't expect it to be any different. The wisdom of God comes only by means of the Spirit of God. Spiritually insensitive people simply cannot see or understand the significance of spiritual gifts and the supremacy of spiritual wisdom. From the perspective of unredeemed society, Christianity will continue to look foolish and Christians will continue to look like fools.

But the evaluation of a secular world is no more than a loudly acclaimed mistaken opinion—even though it may be a majority opinion. "God fixes values without regard to human assessment and according to his own good pleasure."[3] In other words, if God's wisdom looks foolish to people who aren't Christian, that doesn't make it so.

Remarkably, Paul took the worst words the unredeemed Corinthians could hurl at him and accepted them gladly. Yes, he was a fool, but the very meaning of the word had been transformed by the ministry of Christ. For Christians the word *fool* was a term of honor rather than humor, a title of respect rather than repudiation.

From this perspective Paul's boast is understandable. If the gospel of Christ is folly, he is proud to be foolish. If a disciple is a fool, so be it. Paul is pleased to be a part of a fellowship that states straightforwardly and demonstrates openly, "We are fools for Christ's sake!"

Confessional Identity

Correlation between disciples of Christ ("fools for Christ's sake") and clowns in the world is unmistakable. Once again the impact of a word has been transformed.

Etymologically the precise origin of the word *clown* is uncertain. Most likely it sprang from the same root as words such as *clod, clumsy, club,* and *cluster*.[4] Conceptually the noun derived its meaning from the farm workers, or boors, whom townspeople viewed as funny. So a clown was seen as "a funny fellow, a buffoon, a jester."[5]

The word *fool* comes to us from a Latin root *follis,* that in its singular form means "a pair of bellows," "a windbag," and in its plural form denotes "puffed cheeks"—both are descriptive of our historical ideas of a clown.[6] The idea that comes to us from this sketchy review of words and definitions is that persons who don't blend into all that is considered normal and whose ideas don't conform to what society accepts as rational are fools and clowns. We've often heard someone warned against "clowning around": stop being irrational and undignified.

Numerous voices in secular society disgustedly shout "Clown!" at a person who walks outside the proven path to "success"—who reacts to hatred with love, who adopts a way of life that does not conform to acceptable, predictable expectations, and who remains faithful to promises even at a significant financial cost. To today's hardnosed pragmatist a person is a clown who would rather be right than win, who works for peace amid strategists who plan for war, who exercises mercy when others think justice is too demanding, who dreams with expectations of fulfillment, who prays when others panic, and who is unafraid even of death because of a faith that is sure of life. On the surface these "clowns" are irrational, but for a person of faith a higher wisdom is at work.

"Clown!" What is meant by critics as condemnation is accepted by Christians as commendation. Yes, Christians are fools for Christ. Christians are clowns.

Numerous writers have recognized the close relationship between clowns and Christians and recorded their thoughts. And in my pilgrimage for understanding I have read a great deal of what these folks have written.[7] I've studied theological clowns, theatrical clowns, literary clowns, philosophical clowns, and their wide range of comic kin.

But I finally stopped my research with the realization that I was laboring as a slave within the very kind of rationalistic bondage from which true clowns seek to set us free. No carefully structured, artfully phrased, well-reasoned statement is required to prove that clowns are a welcome addition to our world. The youngest child knows that. And, certainly, no heavy theological verbiage is required to document the "foolishness of the Gospel" and the clownlike nature of those who believe it and live by it. We need only to look around attentively and read the Scriptures sensitively to know that. Christians are clowns!

Words from the Polish writer Lesek Kolakowski encourage me. He writes of the philosophy of the jester, "which in every epoch denounces as doubtful what appears as unshakable . . . ridicules common sense into the absurd . . . undertakes the daily toil of the jester's profession along with the inevitable risk of appearing ludicrous."[8] Though Kolakowski is commenting about jesters, he is describing Christians as well. Such an observation causes us to ponder carefully an intriguing question from Frederick Buechner, "Is it possible, I wonder, to say that it is only when you hear the gospel as a wild and marvelous joke that you really hear it at all?"9 Before blurting out, "Yes, yes, that's it!" I find myself wanting to ask if that is not true for *living* the gospel as well. I think so, for I've come to see that only when we live the gospel as free and joyous clowns, do we live it at all.

All right, the point is made. God's kind of people—in biblical terms, the people of God—are the clowns of this world. Now comes the question, Where are they? Where are those kind of people? Where are the clowns?

2. God Calls Them

Either God has a knack for attracting people who, to the world, appear a little odd, or the call of God makes people that way. Almost invariably faithful obedience to a summons from God looks like foolishness from the perspective of this world. Serious believers are frequently confused with buffoons.

Dare we speak of the "foolishness of God" and risk the image of a clownish creator-redeemer? Paul did. In fact, the noted apostle from Tarsus contrasted "what seems to be God's foolishness" with the content of "human wisdom" (1 Cor. 1:25).

There is a great deal of agreement these days with Paul's thinking. Many people continue to question the wisdom, or lack of it, behind the divine selection of the Jews as a "light to the nations" in the Old Testament and the invitation that brought together twelve very different, mostly unpolished, if not often crude, social misfits as disciples of Christ in the New Testament. And there are certainly those who wonder why the Lord entrusted the good news of the gospel and the ministry of redemption to that very human fellowship known, in today's world, as the church.

In the minds of many people, God is needlessly

vulnerable because of his selection of strategy and his choice of servants. Frankly, neither fares very well when measured by the normally accepted standards of contemporary society. We might think that God, being God, could assure more success for his ventures and more popularity for his people. God must love clowns.

Old Testament Clowns

Old Testament writers provide a virtual Who's Who of clowns in the ancient world. Even though we see them as heroes and heroines now, most, if not all, of these people were condemned with laughter by their peers in their cultures.

Think of Noah. Imagine this man feverishly working to complete a boat capable of riding out a surging flood, when such high water never had occurred in the past and not even a hint of bad weather existed in the present. Why, Noah was the funniest story in town. He was the object of ridicule and the butt of cruel jokes. It doesn't stretch our imaginations even a little bit to hear someone saying, "Noah, you clown, have you lost your mind? Suppose you are able to complete your construction and gather all of those animals on board that boat with you. Can you imagine what that will smell like? You must be crazy to want to live under such conditions."

But Noah remained faithful to the Lord's instructions. And next we read that on the very day the ark was loaded and the door shut "all the fountains of the deep burst forth, and the windows of heaven were opened. And rain fell upon the earth forty days and forty nights" (Gen. 7:11–12).

Readers hurrying through the remainder of the Genesis narratives on beginnings are suddenly stopped short, shocked by the account of an old woman laughing hilariously, uproariously. Strangely, no sooner had she laughed than she attempted to deny laughing. But there was no getting out of it. Sarah had laughed. And little wonder. This ninety-year-old woman, at an age appropriate for a great-grandmother, had just been told that within nine months she would give birth to a child—her first. Who would not have laughed? Readers of this story cannot help but be most impressed, though, with who laughed last. Wisely, Sarah realized that ultimately her laughter came from God, the Holy One, even as did the promise of her child. She named her little boy Isaac, a Hebrew word that means "he laughs," so that "everyone who hears about it will laugh" (Gen. 21:6)—with her, not at her.

Can you see a joyous woman who does not look her age clinging lovingly to a newborn child, both of whom are watched over, proudly and protectively, by a doting old male clown named Abraham? This was only the start of a holy history of the people of promise—the beginning of a parade of clowns.

Then there was Moses! Here was a goatkeeper who thought he heard God call him to be a national deliverer; a poor speaker, by his own admission, summoned to become a medium of the divine message. This Israelite who had fled the wrath of an Egyptian king after killing one of his subjects accepted responsibility for speaking to another Egyptian king about the release of all of his Israelite slaves. And commissioning for this task came during a conversation with a burning bush!

Moses easily could have been mistaken for a court jester rather than a holy man in Pharaoh's presence. How the ruler must have laughed—first chuckling at the introductory words of this roughshod shepherd, "The Lord, the God of the Hebrews, sent me to tell you . . . " while thinking "Why would any god speak *to*, much less *through*, this kind of lowly individual?" and then roaring at Moses' audacious demand to let his people go. Who did this fellow think he was? He must be crazy—this clown named Moses.

Actually, many of the best-known Old Testament personalities, highly acclaimed by writers of Scripture, even considered heroes and heroines of the faith, were viewed with derisive skepticism by many of their contemporaries. David stood before Goliath, looking like an ill-equipped midget engaging in battle with a well-armed giant, but thinking he could win.

Later, though, the boy lost his luster. Ironically, the man honored as Israel's ideal king, the one whose name was associated with Bethlehem, the birthplace of Jesus, had been involved in murder and adultery. This major personality in the lineage of Jesus had egg on his face, to say nothing of what had been in his heart. Does that realization speak most pertinently to the clownish nature of God's people or to the foolishness of God?

Jonah was a joke. How strange that a man of God would scurry around looking for a place where he could hide from God, that a messenger of redemption would want the validation of his prophecy of judgment by means of vindictive destruction. Yet, by way of the almost humorous actions of this curious minister, the city of Nineveh was changed and thoughtful readers of the Bible book that bears his name are encouraged toward a vision of faithfulness in missions.

Then there was Job: a beleaguered believer, pathetic

yet heroic, hoping against all odds to the contrary, seeking to make sense of the sores that covered his body, learning that a garbage heap can be a divine altar, and discovering the dynamic presence of God amid the awesome silence of God. Maybe Horace M. Kallen's observation about Job has a general validity as well: "The just, the perfect man is a laughing stock."[1] A clown!

Wherever we look among God's people, clowns come into focus. Consider the prophets.

See Isaiah traipsing around naked and barefoot trying to dramatize the severity of his prophetic message. Listen to a herdsman from Takoa lashing out at religious leaders in the cultic centers of Israel, believing that he possesses a word from God that they have not heard despite their positions of privilege and agenda of prayers and rituals.

Then there is Jeremiah, who provokes tears as well as smiles, comically embracing strange metaphors in his orations and actions. We see him jostling back and forth between prison and palace, refusing to say what people want to hear or to side with a patriotic zeal that is narrowly nationalistic. So few alterations could assure more acceptance for this man from Anathoth. At times it seems as if he wants to be expelled from the nation—shot into the air from some decorated cannon.

Hear Ezekiel if you can. Despite his weird visions that prompt laughs and tempt distrust, this prophet of the exile who sits silently by the River Chebar in Babylon speaks eloquently the message of worldwide redemption.

Was there a clown among the prophets? Actually, that is not the question. More to the point is the inquiry, Was there a single prophet who was not perceived as a clown?

Think of that nameless visionary whose ministry to God's people in captivity was recorded in Isaiah 40–66.

Imagine, in the midst of bondage, while hurting personally, this ancient seer wrote of a day when hurts would be a means of healing. A reading of Isaiah 53 incites hope and nurtures confidence despite a difficult situation by uniting the message of comfort from this prophet clown and the promise of a Savior clown yet to come.

Or remember Hosea, who brings to mind one of those inflatable plastic stand-up punching bags with weights in its rounded bottom and a clown's face painted on its top. Regardless of how hard he was struck or how low he was bent, he kept springing back into an upright position. Was Hosea a fool? Some folks make a strong case for such an opinion.

Hosea persisted in his love for his runaway wife until her protests had stopped and his sensitive care was desperately needed and appreciated, if not openly requested. With every right to retaliate, Hosea refused to denounce the one who betrayed him and continued to love her at her most unlovable worst. What a picture of a clown: Gomer's fool! What an insight into divine compassion! What a revelation of Almighty God!

Of course the issue is much larger than a few individuals. Historically the Jewish people as a group have been the victims of laughter as well as persecution. Self-acclaimed wise persons have questioned God's special covenant relation with the people of Israel. Cryptic lines repeated tongue-in-cheek by some have been embraced in seriousness by others:

> How odd of God
> To choose the Jews.

In one form or another, the question continues to be raised as to why God decided to entrust his divinely ordained work to people who were "just like everyone else but more so."[2] Though biblically described as a "nation of priests," in reality the Israelites more often than not behaved like a fellowship of schlemiels. Yet God calls just such people into the community of the faithful as emissaries of his holy will and witnesses to his gracious salvation.

And if you think people called by God look clownish, you will be amazed at how buffoonish they look before God is finished with them!

Jesus as Clown

Of course the climax of this comic procession of God's called-out people was the coming of Christ. In Jesus of Nazareth, God outdid himself—in reality, revealed himself. This pinnacle of redemptive revelation, the very incarnation of divine wisdom, looked to the world like folly. Whoever would look for the Son of God among a couple of newlyweds, unceremoniously hounded by hurtful rumors and curiously surrounded by a group of despised shepherds, huddled in an animal stall on a back street in a town like Bethlehem!

Reading about clowns leads to thinking about Jesus. Samuel Miller describes the clown in contemporary art as a character in whom "various worlds collide," an individual whose "excessive exaggeration and gross simplicity touches the hem of the metaphysical, that realm which tends to be smothered in ages proud of their pragmatic and utilitarian efficiency."[3] Strangely, when devotees of such art discover the clown standing at the intersection of the two worlds, they hear laughter and realize the necessity of both worlds.

Was that why angels sang joyfully at Jesus' birth and Simeon hummed confidently when he saw the long-awaited child at the temple? Surely Jesus was the personal nexus of time and eternity, historical herald of the advent of the Kingdom of God amid the kingdoms of this world. And it was through this Jesus that the invitation came for people to live so freely and happily because of their salvation, causing distant observers to scoff foolishly from their one-dimensional situations.

Little wonder that Jesus has been described as a clown. Out of the comic absurdity of their situation, the catacomb Christians of the first century made the identification of Christ as a clown. George Rouault was the first to make the association explicit in modern times. The movie called *The Parable* and the play called *Godspell* dramatize this notion about Christ that had previously been confined primarily to the printed page. Artists have been more bold. One of the earliest paintings of the crucifixion displays the head of a jackass atop the abused body of Jesus. The artist's comment seems obvious: Christ is a fool; how senseless to live as he lived so as to die as he died!

No doubt some people immediately recoil from such talk and sense a discomforting closeness to sacrilege. We'd better not be too hasty in that kind of response though. Both from biblical literature and personal experience comes a hint that something about this image of Jesus rings true. At the center of the association between Jesus and clowns is a promise of something profoundly important.

Colin Morris suggests that the gospel narratives on Jesus' life constitute "a Clown's Progress," the documentation of a developmental relationship between this clown from Nazareth and the laughter that he provoked.[4] Actually, so much of the life and ministry of Jesus can be considered a "burlesque of the sacred"[5] that the journey of Jesus as a clown deserves careful attention.

First, people laughed with Jesus. Consistently, Christ's humor was a positive, constructive component of his ministry. But he never evoked laughter to hurt a person or to poke fun at a group. Humor was a servant of redemptive truth that he employed to clarify, to encourage, and to enlighten.

What a storyteller! Images of truth were conveyed so delightfully by Jesus that often realizations of truth were emblazoned in his listeners' consciences; and these realizations were accompanied by smiles. Laughter and wisdom, good humor and compassionate concern were wed in his words. Those who heard and understood, laughed and learned.

Buechner may well be right in thinking that "more often than not the parables can be read as high and holy jokes about God and about man and about the gospel itself as the highest and holiest joke of them all."[6] Like a good joke teller, Jesus often refused to elaborate on the meaning of the stories that he told. In a sense, explanation of the stories compromised both the message and the medium. Most crucial to Jesus' intent was not the listeners' grasp of every minute detail in his narratives but their realization of the redemptive truth revealed in them.

Nowhere is the humor of Jesus more apparent than in the appeal to absurdity that marks so many of his parables. Some of the language of Jesus has lost its comical spirit in the translations of terms and in the differences between cultures. But many of his word-pictures continue to communicate powerfully, humorously.[7]

Jesus talked of a camel passing through the eye of a needle. Listeners imagined the incredible contortions attempted by this awkward-looking beast of burden trying to negotiate an impossible passage, and suddenly, while smiling, caught a glimpse of truth about the relationship between material riches and spiritual commitment. Jesus described the kind of people who walked around with wooden planks protruding from their eyes while criticizing other people who had specks of sawdust caught in their eyes. The hilarity of the imagery was related to the severity of judgment.

My guess is that people thoroughly enjoyed informal times of fellowship with Jesus. Surely laughter could have been heard among those who walked with Jesus, who rubbed elbows with him during a daytime journey along a Galilean road, as well as among those who enjoyed the intimacy of an evening meal with him.

Predictably, some folks felt that Jesus enjoyed life too much. Seeming to fear that laughter was irreligious and that associating with sinners was the same as sinning, these pseudo-pietists wanted Jesus' circle of relationships narrowed. For them, even the appearance of frivolity was to be replaced with fasting, and any hint of lighthearted joy among his followers was to be preempted by a depression that could be mistaken for devotion. Of course such a reaction is the best indication that Jesus was the type of person with whom fellowship was genuinely joyful as well as profoundly meaningful. He knew how to live abundantly. In fact, the good humor in his teaching was naturally compatible with the good spirit of his living. People laughed with Jesus.

Sadly, the day came when people laughed *at* Jesus. Scorn and scoffing replaced smiles among many of those who listened to him carefully and watched him intently. The satisfying laughs of serendipitous experiences gave way to the sardonic chuckles of heinous plots and plans. Robust enjoyment eroded; ridicule, slander, and indictments took its place.

At work here is an important transformation of terms. Though initially much appreciated for the stories he told, eventually Jesus was much maligned for the meanings that these stories conveyed as well as for his manner of ministry. Those who labeled him as foolish intended no goodwill. For persons who evaluated Jesus from a secular perspective or from a narrowly sectarian point of view, he looked and sounded clownish. The judgment was passed with harsh displeasure, even disgust. Now, today, to praise him as a clown is to turn a phrase—to, in retrospect, recognize the honor of a dishonorable term.

The more Jesus talked about the Kingdom of God, the more discomfort many people experienced. Gripped by Jesus' words about the long-awaited messianic banquet, students of the Scriptures were troubled by Jesus' guest list. To this unique meal for the redeemed, Jesus would invite thieves and murderers, poor people and prostitutes, crippled folks and blinded individuals, and even nonreligious persons—a most motley group of table guests. A summons to the supper from Jesus would be sent to crude shacks along the roadside as well as to the temple. Surely this man must be out of his mind. What a clown!

Imagine people listening to Jesus speak—nervously shifting their weight from one foot to another, mulling over his message in their minds, later questioning his wisdom by examining it in the light of their tradition, and finally concluding with deep conviction that he must be belittled, refuted, maybe killed. To them his reasoning was tragically distorted.

Jesus actually commended the behavior of a shepherd who looked patiently and lovingly for one lost sheep though he had the other ninety-nine members of his flock locked safely in the fold. Commending such a reaction to a dumb sheep was no more ridiculous, though, than praising a father who joyously welcomed home a wayward son. Instead of seeing to it that this young scoundrel received his proper putdown and administering a heavy punishment, the father joyously welcomed him home, forgave him freely, and celebrated the homecoming with a banquet. And Jesus praised that! Just as the son made a fool of the father, affirmation of this story made a fool of its teller.

Did Jesus not understand the ways of the world? Surely not, or else he would not have devoted so much time to poor people despised by others, offered forgiveness to individuals whom society would have stoned, and proclaimed a message that created controversy and crisis. Evidently Jesus never learned how to hedge his bets, play things close to the chest. Rather, he stated his love unequivocally and extended grace vulnerably.

No wonder people laughed at Jesus and eventually killed him. This world understands power, partisanship, retribution, compromise, and less than the best. Whoever heard of praying for your enemies, much less turning both cheeks to be slapped by them? Repaying evil with good is nothing more than a foolish means of going broke and getting abused. Most people are just not worth the price to be paid in faithfulness to that kind of selfless morality. Colin Morris puts the matter succinctly: "If the decision to choose for love in a world such as this is strictly the act of a clown, then Jesus was the biggest fool in history."[8]

As we examine with greater care the words and teachings of Jesus, the parallels between the teacher from Galilee and clowns stretch toward infinity.

Typically the teachings of a clown are foolish to the wise. Perhaps the clown's truths are appreciated as long as they are confined to a ring under a circus tent, but they are not to be tolerated if any broader application is attempted. A person may speak of anxiety by talk of flowers in the fields and birds in the air as long as such a response is identified as fanciful entertainment. But such palaver has no place in markets of commerce, houses of legislation, offices of vocational counsel, or strategy rooms of military brass. And how dare any employer offer one set wage to different persons who had worked shifts of various lengths! More than the labor unions would be upset at such a policy. Individuals, like institutions, relate best to and respond to the language of hard bargains, not to talk about grace. Jesus the clown!

Both as a figure in literature and as an actual entertainer in some show, the clown is often homeless, transient. Not only does the clown function apart from the security of any one place called home, a question exists as to whether acceptance would be sufficient anywhere to assure a permanent residence even if it were desired. Listen to this matter-of-fact statement of the carpenter from Nazareth turned minister to the world: "The Son of Man has nowhere to lay his head." Jesus the clown!

Usually an aura of mystery surrounds a clown. When is the clown serious and when is he only kidding? When is the clown playfully acting and when is she really exhorting? Is he basically a little boy or a mature man? Is she honestly a small girl or a grown woman?

William Willeford's words about the fool, particularly the religious fool, are pertinent: The fool "is neither child nor man in St. Paul's sense but both and something else"—a person with "a pure and unwavering reaction to the mystery of 'eternal things.'"⁹ People recognize just enough of themselves in the clown's nature to be attracted, but then quickly turn away when too severely challenged by a recognition of the presence of higher values and a hint of transcendence. Jesus walked the boundary between two worlds. Jesus the clown!

Frequently, by one of the quirks of human tendencies, clowns are jokingly acclaimed or scornfully assailed as royalty. Admittedly, their regal vestments are ludicrous and their thrones as well as their fiefdoms are absurd. I wonder, did those first-century Roman soldiers who drew the crucifixion detail on a Passover weekend sense that they were in charge of a sovereign fool? Jesus the clown!

Invariably clowns appear to know something that not all people know. How else can you explain their irresponsible joy and hope? Admirably, a clown can bound back when knocked down, and even when apparently blocked will continue happily on his or her way.

More than one writer has been impressed with a kinship between the character traits of Charlie Chaplin and those of Jesus of Nazareth. Reflecting on Jesus' somber words to his disciples about having to die and go away but then come again, Buechner wrote, "The great confidence in these words of Jesus is like the twirl of a cane and the twitch of a mustache as the little tramp stands there so jaunty and hopeful in his baggy pants while the whole world threatens to fall on him like a pail of water balanced on top of a door."[10]

Predictably, people finally passed a point of no return in their on-again, off-again relationship with Jesus. A laughter that had been perhaps an annoyance became a mockery that would kill him. Those persons who had positioned themselves as opponents of Jesus and laughed loudest at him wanted to be sure that they laughed last. This clown must die! He is dangerous. For the good of society, and for his own good really, he must be silenced.

For a while all laughter ceased—even the dirty guttural rumblings that accompany a sinister scenario successfully played out. This Jesus-thing was far too serious for any diversion. In fact, not until Jesus was a captive could his detractors poke fun, mock, and laugh again. But once he was safely in their hands, a new kind of gaiety erupted.

Near the end, which turned out to be the beginning, the clown was treated as a clown. Thorns were thrust onto his head. Laugh at his regal crown! A cross was placed in his hands. Look at his scepter! A parade with the clownish king at its center twisted its way through the narrow lanes of the holy city, accompanied by the jeers, taunts, and curses of unholy people.

At a crucifixion site beside a garbage dump outside Jerusalem's gates, the sometimes-supposed savior of the world, the widely acclaimed fool, was attached to a splintery throne and raised above the crowd so he could die looking at his kingdom: a small plot of earth with features that reminded its visitors of a skull. Now the hilarity peaked. At last they had him in his place. Here was where he belonged. Jests encouraged the joviality.

"Why don't you come down, King?" "Surely you can call some angels to help you, holy man."

Those in charge of the crucifixion judged the joke too good to be missed by anyone. So they printed it in three languages: King of the Jews.

One writer dares to wonder if the clown is "perhaps himself the laughter of the Infinite about the Finite when it pretends to be absolute."[11] Maybe, quite honestly, though, a reading of the pilgrimage of the clown from Nazareth leaves us with a question about who is laughing.

Most obvious are the people around the cross. Many of them are laughing. They have made their point about the place of God-infected people in this world. Raw power has won out over humble compassion. Servanthood has been rebuffed as a valid way of life. Tradition has been preserved. Legality has been protected and perpetuated as morality. The clown who thought he could change all of this is dying, or dead. They are laughing.

But other sounds confuse any quick conclusions. Thunder rolls across the skies, like the waves of a high tide swept by a strong wind crash into the sands of a shoreline. Lightning cracks in the air, like the rush of fire sweeping swiftly through a dead tree.

Who do these people clustered around the cross think they are? Have finite creatures dared to imagine themselves as possessors of infinite wisdom? Sure, Jesus looked like a clown; he was God's clown. But was he God's laughter? Is that the other sound to be heard here? Knowing the difference between the laughter of God—so deep, rich, and full—and the laughter of people who think they can control God—so shallow, bankrupt, and fake—is knowing the difference between life and death.

God liked what he saw in Jesus Christ, and he would

not allow this kind of joy to die. The redeeming clown must live. So after three days of the tears of heartbreak among some and the nervous laughter of an uncertain security among others—resurrection!

Jesus was alive. The clown lives. An invitation into his fellowship persists. Salvation by means of his love continues. God wants more people patterned after him. What God did in Christ he desires to do in others. The pilgrimage of the Son of God is to be the pilgrimage of all of the children of God. Remember, Jesus the clown said over and over, "Follow me."

Not only has God called clowns, God calls clowns. The divine will intends a clown parade in the present. So today, where are they? Where are the clowns?

3. The Gospel Shapes Them

Fidelity to the gospel of Christ produces persons who appear to the world either as mad or foolish—culturally unwise if not clinically insane. The message transforms its messengers. Gospel-oriented beliefs are complemented by gospel-shaped behavior.

Of course people who live apart from the gospel don't understand persons who live daily by God's good news. Christians function on the basis of a completely different set of values and espouse a radically different worldview. This simply means that persons who from a Christian perspective look and act like faithful followers of Christ give the appearance from a secular perspective of being comical clowns.

No one knew this truth better than the Apostle Paul. Former friends and colleagues laughed at the reported conversion of this citizen from Tarsus and ridiculed his altered way of life. Festus, a well-known political official, openly accused Paul of being crazy. Athenian philosophers laughingly scorned both the man and his message. The apostle to the Gentiles knew full well the cost of life-changing convictions. In fact, when he wrote to the Christians at Corinth about the gospel being folly, he was in reality writing autobiography. Read carefully and thoughtfully the tentmaker's personal confession, "We are fools for Christ's sake." We are clowns! The gospel will do that to a person every time.

Not surprisingly, devotion to the clownish Christ produced disciples who looked like clowns. In fact, the clown parade in the New Testament started even prior to the birth of Jesus.

John the Baptist was praised by Jesus as one greater than any man who has ever lived (Matt. 11:11). But heaven only knows all of the other tags that were attached to this strange prophet. In his singleminded obedience to God and undeviating commitment to his task, John the Baptist came off looking like a clown. In all probability even those who liked John personally and responded to his message positively were amused at times by his dress, diet, and demeanor. John was right at home with those divinely commissioned schlemiels of the Old Testament known as prophets. But, as Jesus indicated, he stood above them.

Mary was another story. On the basis of one conversation with an angel—an event that in retrospect could have been dismissed as a hallucination provoked by heat, fatigue, or stress—risked her promised union with Joseph and her established reputation in the community.

Based on that conversation, though, Mary reordered her life. In the midst of false rumors crudely gossiped about her and untrue accusations insensitively leveled at her, Mary made music. She gave herself to a celebration prompted by a vision of promise and redemption.

How very much like a clown! Though at times apparently rebuffed and frequently confused, Mary never wavered in her commitment to Jesus. When the final joke about Jesus was posted above his crucified body, Mary was as near to her son as she could get. Only now she stood by him also because he was her Lord. What kind of foolishness was this?

Once Jesus actually appeared on the scene, clowns seemed to come out of the woodwork. When presented at the temple for his circumcision, the baby Jesus was surrounded by an elderly man and woman who reacted to him as though they were his new parents, talked about him as though they were young evangelists, and believed that having witnessed his presence they could then die in peace. Surely passersby must have stopped and looked at the commotion with amazement or shook their heads and walked on with condescending (or maybe envying) smiles.

These same kinds of responses accompanied Jesus' public ministry. How people must have snickered as Zacchaeus—a short, dignified public official—set image aside and scaled a tree in order to see Jesus. Have you ever watched a clown dressed in a tuxedo walk around on stilts? But if Zacchaeus looked funny going up the tree, he must have provoked even more merriment coming down. Suddenly this little scoundrel wanted to right his wrongs, even to repay fourfold those persons whom he had cheated. Can you imagine? People who knew him laughed. But this conniving clown discounted the egg on his face, disdained what people would say, and resolved to be a friend to Jesus.

At times Jesus' uniqueness was recognized most readily by folks whom society considered deranged. At other times people were considered strange and insane because they readily recognized uniqueness in Jesus.

Without doubt, in any contest to select the most humorous of Jesus' followers, the twelve disciples would, together, take first place. Repeatedly these diverse individuals matured and regressed, learned of humility and longed for greatness, developed in devotion and harbored doubts. They prayed for peace and quarreled among themselves, believed the best and feared the worst, accepted servanthood and aspired to sovereignty, vowed their faithfulness no matter what transpired and wavered before difficulties ever emerged. And while walking the dusty Palestine roads, the disciples listened to the master teacher and failed to understand his truth.

Even the gospel writers poked fun at these disciples. But despite their stumbling and bumbling, when all was said and done, at least eleven of them staked their lives on the conviction that the world could be changed by the one whom they followed. Actually, the twelfth member of the group may have believed the same thing, but he wanted his leader to be a mighty king rather than a clown.

Peter epitomized the disciple-clown. This fiery fisher's natural impulsiveness was enough to make people convulse in laughter even before his spiritual conversion gave him an infusion of enthusiasm. Hear Peter's bold assertions of intention reverberate against the backdrop of his weak, waffling will. See Peter in one moment fearlessly stepping across the waves of a stormy sea in order to meet his Lord and then in the very next moment fearfully flailing away at the water in order to keep from drowning. Peter was always adamant—whether in faithfulness, confessing Jesus as Lord at Caesarea-Philippi, or in unfaithfulness, denying any knowledge of Jesus by a campfire in Jerusalem.

How could Jesus speak of such a man as a potential leader in the church? Did he want a buffoon priest? Then, as if this declarative disciple did not act insanely enough in the course of his life, Peter used his death to make a point emphatically. Refusing to submit to a simple crucifixion, Peter requested that he be attached to his cross upside down. This unmistakably clownish act, though, was a vivid illustration of Peter's devotion to and respect for his Lord, and at the same time, it was the fulfillment of Jesus' prediction at the lakeside about Peter's death (John 21:19).

"We are fools for Christ's sake." Any one of hundreds of people in the first-century world could have written this confession. Paul was not alone. Jesus attracted, encouraged, and commissioned this kind of disciple. He still does.

In writing to the Christians at Corinth, Paul explains what happens. "If anyone is in Christ, he is a new creation; the old has passed away. Behold, the new has come." (2 Cor. 5:17). Conversion! A new creation! True, but to unchanged people of the world Christians made new by Christ appear clownish. Paul was familiar with the digs of secular society. He knew what people were thinking and saying, so in his direct way he offered a personal response that applied equally to Christians in every century: "For if we are beside ourselves [insane], it is for God [it is for God's sake]" (2 Cor. 5:13).

It was for "God's sake" then, and it is the same now. But people still misunderstand. To much of the world, authentic Christianity looks like absolute insanity. Christians are clowns.

Today, then, where are the clowns? Answering that question requires a detailed understanding of the people we're looking for. And to achieve that understanding, we need to take a close look at those attributes of belief and characteristics of behavior that are held in common by Christians and clowns. That very exercise, by the way, documents the fascinating fact that the gospel shapes precisely the kind of person, both ideologically and behaviorally, who conforms most completely to the image of a clown. Consider the parallels.

Clowns are vulnerable lovers who find great joy in giving. Clowns actually prefer giving to receiving. Watch them. Happiness spreads across the grease-painted face of a clown who gives away two hundred balloons and a sack of candy. Never is there even the slightest thought of keeping back something for herself. Clowns live to give. In fact, living is enhanced for clowns when attention is focused only on them. But clowns want attention drawn to themselves only in order to perform better for others.

Clowns are at their best when making others feel important. Watch a shaggy-haired old clown offer a bouquet of flimsy, gaudy crepe-paper flowers to a bright-eyed little girl. Her pleasure is the reward of clowning. Whether onlookers laugh at or cry over a clown, they know that the clown has been attentive to them, performed for them, and sought a place of affection within them.

Obviously extreme vulnerability is part of a clown's life. Yet clowns opt for the risks of close-up love rather than for the security of detached reason. Not that reason and love must be opposites, but the order of the two is important. Primary here is not a reasoned love but a loving reason—not love in the service of reason but reason subservient to love. Clowns are totally disinterested in calculating the costs of their commitments of compassion or in figuring the returns on investments of their love.

Vulnerability is essential in the nature of a clown.

Without it a clown would be devoid of the capacity for selfless love. For this reason clowns make no attempt to repress, alleviate, or hedge their vulnerability. They are bent toward love regardless of the benefits or liabilities involved.

What images are brought to mind by this description?

A parade clown pausing in front of crowded bleachers and stretching to reach three rows back in order to hand a piece of bubble gum to a shy little boy. And all the while he suffers the potential danger of having his big red nose tweaked or his padded stomach punched or his puffy sleeves torn.

A frolicking rodeo clown stalking a maddened bull, knowing that he could as easily get hurt as cause laughter, but realizing that a thrown cowboy is in danger and a crowd of people is wanting to be entertained.

An old gray-haired man named John on the island of Patmos continuing to write about the necessity of faithful love and durable commitment even though it is those very attributes that are the reason for his own persecution and imprisonment.

A young Christian named Stephen falling under a barrage of stones while witnessing to his faith and praying for the forgiveness of the people who are killing him.

Most certainly our images of Christians and clowns get all mixed up as we ponder the puzzle of vulnerable lovers who find great joy in giving.

Then, too, precedent apparently means little to a clown. Clowns refuse to be convinced by history. Plenty of evidence points to the conclusion that in this world love gets betrayed, promises are broken, truth is attacked, and commitments are compromised. Not to recognize this reality is to risk being used, getting dumped on, or being taken for a ride. But clowns will not listen to such talk. Clowns persist in what they believe most and do best: loving and giving. Incidentally, so do Christians.

Faithfulness to your beliefs, like rightness in your actions, is not dependent on a recognition of it or applause for it. Vulnerable lovers are belittled as incurable clowns. (Remember the old country song "Cathy's Clown"?) For some reason people think that a person is foolish for continuing to love despite setbacks, hardships, or betrayals from the one loved.

Do not believe it. Real love is not dependent on a reciprocal love. Similarly, selfless giving frequently is labeled as senseless living. Obviously society much prefers maximum benefits and minimum risks in every endeavor. Thankfully, clowns—and Christians—will have none of that kind of reasoning. Both really believe in love: that people can be loved; that people can be loving; that love can melt coldness, eradicate harshness, and alter selfishness; that love can find more joy in giving than in getting. And both the Christian and the clown have the bruises to prove it.[1]

Clowns are incurable dreamers who refuse to be deterred by great challenges. Clowns live by dreaming. What makes a small, grinning, prankster whose path is blocked by an elephant pop a broom against the tough backside of that overpowering animal and think she can get away with it? Surely the answer to that question must be related to an explanation of why a chubby, wobbly-walking imitator of an officer of the law can hold up his white-gloved, oversized hand to an onrushing stunt car with confidence that it will skid to a halt—within an inch of his face.

Clowns seem either incapable of comprehending the

danger of various situations or unaware of the impossibil-
ity of their endeavors. Not even failing in one attempt or
getting hurt in another is enough to cause a clown to stop
clowning. Do clowns just not know that certain problems
cannot be solved and some goals cannot be achieved? Or
do they see something that other people fail to see?

Dreams determine the life map of a clown. But a
clown's dreams do not constitute a cop-out. Just the
opposite. Such visions lead to encounters. A clown lives
out his dreams. A clown who dreams of a different world
will not settle for less, thus refusing to make himself
comfortable in this world. Visions of better people lead to
actions aimed at making people better. In every instance
the strength of the dream within a clown is sufficient to
withstand contradictions, setbacks, and disappointments.
A clown lives from the inside out!

How familiar to students of the Christian gospel are
the sight, sound, and spirit of such a life! Prophetic
dreams of people came in the midst of war. Visions of
reordering the world developed when everything seemed
to be deteriorating. Massive poverty did not prevent
efforts toward economic justice.

Vision is essential to living, not a luxury for escaping.
Dreams are meant for translation into specific programs.
Priestly convictions about a faith that can move mountains
is not confined to level ground. Confidence in the
sufficiency of salvation for any situation removes any fear
of suffering, hesitancy because of discouraging odds, or
reticence because of negative precedents.

Think of those men in funny-looking hoods living in
celibacy, working in the fields, reading the Scriptures, and
actually believing that their prayers of intercession can
produce change in the world. Monks they are called. Or is

it clowns? How nonsensical it seemed both at the time and now in retrospect: a black preacher standing on the steps of the Lincoln Memorial, surrounded by a scared and angered society, speaking to an audience participating in a march of the poor. How clownish of him to think that a rabid racism so firmly entrenched in the hearts of people and the fabric of society could be altered, much less abolished, with any immediacy. The recollection of that image brings to mind other images: a ludicrous-looking clown ridiculously taking on the challenge of taming a cage full of wild animals; a comedian attempting to bring an onrushing locomotive to a halt with the wave of his hand. But hear him out; the black man explains his behavior by a vision: "I have a dream," he thunders.

If dreams motivate a clown, dreams also sustain a clown. From dreams come direction for action and encouragement for going on. Samuel H. Miller sees this clearly: "Dreams repair the dignity of a clown who has been attacked, castigated, or dismissed. Dreams provide the source of a smile even in the midst of trouble."[2] What the clown sees allows her demeanor not to be determined by the behavior of other people or by the judgments of culture.

Paul's words take on a new ring of relevance at this point: "Do not be conformed to this world but be transformed by the renewing of your mind" (Rom. 12:2). Robert Kennedy puts it this way: "Some people see things as they are and ask why. Others dream of things that never were and ask why not."

Clowns are authors of surprise who bring insight through the unexpected. Surprise is stock in trade for clowns. Wide-eyed, dodging spectators nervously watch one clown pour half a bucket of water on another clown and then toss the remaining contents of the container toward them. Amazingly, however, confetti suddenly has replaced water. A small, bug-shaped car that at most could hold only five average-sized adults speeds into an arena, stops with a screech, and unloads fifteen clowns. A big black hat becomes, in the hands of a clown, a hatchery for rabbits. Surprise!

By no means are all clown surprises confined to circuses. That amusing troubadour in a purple tuxedo who reaches for a coat-pocket handkerchief and pulls and pulls until he has unfolded a silk sheet ten yards long has nothing over that imposing patriarch whose staff became a snake in the Egyptian pharaoh's court. And a little later it was that same bold leader who guided his people in a dramatic escape to freedom that involved the last-minute parting of a body of water just when it looked like the entire exodus entourage either would be killed by Egyptians or drowned in the Red Sea. Then, too, imagine if you can the awesome surprise of the crowd when a loving Savior picked up five loaves and two pieces of fish, blessed the handful of food, and it became a dinner that satisfied more than five thousand people.

There are times when patience is required while watching clowns. Unexpected events may follow at some distance behind the expected. Children inch forward to the edges of their seats as they watch a clown dance her way across a room and assume a position directly under a precariously hung, already sagging chandelier. Every observer can anticipate what is going to happen. And it does. A beautiful light fixture crashes onto the crown of the clown's head, and she crumbles to the floor in a heap. That doesn't seem funny. But wait. After a few moments of hush, the clown stirs a bit, rubs her head, assumes a dazed look, gets up, checks the ceiling for other dangerous objects, and begins to dance again. Onlookers sigh and then laugh.

How different is that clownish antic from action spawned by a gospel-shaped conscience? One man is angry at another, really angry. Anyone can see a fight coming. Then it happens. Anger explodes in a fury that includes a hard slap to the face. A stunned expression crosses the face of the person who was hit, and observers brace for his predictable response. After a few moments that seem like hours, the man with the imprint of a hand on his right cheek turns his left cheek toward his attacker, waits briefly, and then walks away. The fool! No, the disciple: a follower of the One who taught that when slapped on one cheek, a person should turn the other cheek rather than retaliate.

Author Enid Welsford beautifully describes one such clown: "He is none the worse for his slapping, often he turns the tables on the slappers, but sometimes he shrugs his shoulders and inquires: 'What do slaps matter to me, since I can render them not only innocuous but lucrative and funny?' "³ This characterization is wonderfully accurate for all kinds of clowns—the moral and spiritual ones as well as the theatrical and literary ones.

Clowns confront apparent no-win situations as a matter of routine. William Willeford perceives such engagements as clowns dealing with "impossible possibilities—with what, on the one hand, *might be* but, on the other, *is not,* because for one reason or another, it *cannot be.*"⁴ Yet that is not the whole story. More often than not, clowns are victorious in these very predicaments. Tragedies are averted and victories won.

Perhaps someone may wonder what, if anything, all of this has to do with miracles. Good thought. Could it be that miracles are merely the surprises that occur in the lives of the clowns of God?

Swift changes in action that provoke sudden laughter can result in a lasting insight. Not always, of course. Sometimes there is only laughter. At other moments, though, there is more. An unexpected conclusion to what was considered a predictable situation prompts a spontaneous declaration of, "Oh, yeah, now I see!" For some, such surprise can serve as a beneficial type of "shock" therapy.

Life is not predictable! To believe that existence proceeds only according to an inflexible pattern is to ignore both the goings-on of clowns and the teachings of the Bible. Surprise is a part of the very substance of life. Otherwise forgiveness for sins would be unattainable, anxiety followed by peace unthinkable, hatred resolved in reconciliation unachievable, and evil followed by good impossible.

Neither a Christian nor a clown ever will be caught declaring, "That is impossible!" Both kinds of people have learned, each in her own way, that life has far more potential than is acknowledged by any one person. A gospel writer, castigated by some as a clown, said it best: "With God all things are possible." Remember a crucified Savior resurrected as the living Lord? Surprise!

Frequently interruptions are more important than that which is interrupted. Though this realization usually is most helpful only in retrospect, it is nevertheless well worth embracing. Through the unexpected, revelation occurs; truth is conveyed and recognized in a manner unattainable in the expected. To love when hatred is anticipated and to pray for enemies when convention dictates retaliation are actions akin to smiling while getting up from a fall, to giving a piece of candy to a person who has acted ugly, or to pulling a bouquet of flowers out of the ragged back pocket of some baggy pants. Each act represents an unexpected turn of events. All such behavior is surprising—a little bit clownish and a whole lot Christian.

Hope is the ultimate product of this perspective on life. Never is a situation devoid of the possibility of change. Surprise, miracle, or interruption—call it what you will—is not only imaginable but possible. Just ask any clown.

Clowns are resilient copers who resist the limitations of ordinary circumstances. In Heinrich Böll's novel *The Clown,* a disgusted father explains to his son, who is a clown, "You lack the very thing that makes a man a man: the ability to accept a situation."[5] Though errant in his understanding of human nature, the father does perceive correctly the character of a clown, and of a Christian. How true to the essence of the Christian gospel are those persons who refuse to surrender to the givens imposed by a situation. So what if their colleagues counsel otherwise and call them clowns? Fools—religious and otherwise—simply seek either to alter circumstances or to rise above them.

Any clown worth her salt knows how and when to suspend the rules. Sweeping is supposed to be a drab experience. Everyone knows that. Yet a clown can saunter around in circles sweeping—sweeping dirt, sweeping air, sweeping anything—and cause a crowd to roar with delight. What is attractive about a man bending over to tie his shoelace? Nothing. But most people have laughed heartily while watching a clown dramatically topple head over heels into a somersault in his awkward attempt to tie a shoestring. A clown is capable of making something unusual out of the very usual.

Adaptability is a primary attribute of any clown. Although some people are severely threatened, if not completely immobilized, when life does not go as planned or expected, or when problems prevent compliance with normal routines, or when difficulties necessitate experiential detours—not so with a clown.

Watch a clown take part in a downhill skiing contest. He attempts all of the same movements and tries all of the same tricks as other competitors, but something goes wrong in every instance. Rather than serenely swishing past the finish line in a blaze of glory, the clown skier can be seen tumbling down the whitened hillside like a runaway snowball, feet kicking in the air, skis sliding askew, and goggles flying. Failure? No. Onlookers laugh with glee rather than feel pity or sense defeat. A flair accompanies even an act that flirts with dismal failure. The clown succeeds because people are entertained. And so with exaggerated aplomb he picks up his skis, straightens his iridescent ski suit, and, putting on his goggles again, apparently undaunted, the clown heads back up the mountain.

Clowns move with events—ordered or chaotic, expected or unpredicted, easy or difficult. These evokers of laughter seem mystically in touch with the rhythms of nature and the design of God. If a seldom-used detour is better than a well-traveled path and if evasion is more suitable than an encounter, that's all right.

Clowns go on their way—whatever way that is—not

kicking and screaming because of the givens imposed, but whistling and smiling because of the potential to be realized. Winning can come out of losing, success out of failure. By the way, isn't that way of life very close to the life principle that is so basic to the New Testament and so out of place in the world? Jesus states it succinctly, "For whoever would save his life will lose it; and whoever loses his life for my sake and the gospel's will save it" (Mark 8:35).

Sometimes clowns cope best with situations by not coping. They simply refuse to allow limitations to be imposed upon them. And at times clowns seem either unaware of or unconcerned with even the normal restraints of time and space and of law and order. Whether their behavior stems nobly from stubbornness mixed with resilience or merely from a lack of common sense, fools really do rush in where angels (and almost everyone else) fear to tread.

Basically clowns are actors—initiators of action—rather than reactors—responders to action. Often they deal with situations by refusing to accept prescribed boundaries and to comply with designated responses, thus creating a wholly different situation.

Having received a doctor's diagnosis of terminal illness, a patient asserts boldly, "I'm not going to accept that. I'll show you that life can continue." And it does. When informed that no funds are available to support her ministry, a missionary volunteer declares, "I'll begin anyway." And she does.

Far more is involved here than wishful thinking. In fact this approach to life is very much akin to the consequence of obedience to the New Testament admonitions about living as salt and light in the world. Flavor and zest can be added to a tasteless existence. Light can dispel darkness. Physical laws and social proprieties aren't all there is. Life consists also of moral convictions and spiritual strength. You don't have to be victimized by situations. A clown certainly refuses such confinement.

Oh, to be sure, risk is involved. But accepting risk may be the very best means of changing a troublesome situation. Failure as measured by one set of standards may well be judged success when evaluated by different criteria. That is why Harvey Cox is correct both when he observes that a clown is constantly defeated, tricked, and humiliated and when he declares that a clown is "infinitely vulnerable, but never finally defeated."[6]

Clowns are persons of paradox who reside on the boundaries of life. Describing a clown is as tricky as riding a unicycle or walking a tightrope. Just when you've attempted to precisely identify her, you realize that she is also a completely different character. Wolfgang M. Zucker explains the difficulty involved: "Self-contradiction, indeed, is the clown's most significant feature."[7] In whatever way a clown is pictured, the opposite traits can also be used to describe her.

Think of clowns generally or consider any one clown specifically. Immediately both hilarity and sobriety come to mind, as do detachment and empathy, laughter and tears, devious pranks and unselfish helpfulness.

At one moment a clown appears to be quite ordinary, and in the very next instant that same clown seems quite spectacular. Zucker, a careful student of clowns, concludes that each one is "crude and mean, but also gentle and magnanimous, clumsy and inept, but, simultaneously, incredibly agile and endowed with astonishing skills; ugly and repulsive, yet not without elegance and attractive charm."[8]

Is a clown the mixed-up result of some life process that can be likened to the workings of an ambivalent committee? Does a clown represent futile attempts to fuse irreconcilable differences in human experience, to join incompatible traits of individual personalities? Does a clown exist as a compromise character, a pathetic performer seeking to walk a middle way among competing life postures? No. No to each question.

Clowns are persons of paradox in whom a new way of life finds embodiment. They aren't weaklings or nervous social chameleons. Clowns are people of strength who choose to live on the boundaries of life.

Clowns live where two worlds clash—in a literary sense where truth rubs against fiction, in a theatrical sense at the intersection of reality and imagination, and in a theological sense on the boundary between human society and the Kingdom of God. Just when a clown seems totally incredible, some act establishes her as unmistakably one of us. Yet no clown is exactly like any other clown or anyone else.

Most clowns have a strong sense of present reality. Though they may not look or act like it, these festive folks know the nature of life as experienced by everyone else. At the same time, however, another reality is apparent to them: the reality of another world impinging on this one, questioning this one, judging this one.

If clowns did not choose to live on the periphery of life, most likely more "rational" people would relegate them to the outer edges of reality anyway. Don't people assume that clowns can't make it on the streets or succeed in business suits or win approval for public office? They have their proper place. Cultural counsel is familiar: It's best not to confuse two worlds. Deal with only one reality at a time. Life is more predictable that way. Clowns belong in circuses—or in churches.

Is it any surprise that Christians have been called clowns? True disciples of Christ are boundary people—citizens of two worlds who live on the frontier of each.

Traditional values are regularly questioned and frequently reordered by real clowns. What many people accept as self-evident, clowns hold in question. A clown may denounce as doubtful what others have assumed is unshakable. One fictitious jester puts it this way: "Those things which other people call nonfiction seem very fictitious to me."9 Social mores and majority opinions are not to be confused with ethical absolutes and allowed to define moral priorities for periphery persons. Often moral faithfulness may be judged by society as ludicrous. Clowns adopt rules and affirm practices different from those of most of their contemporaries.

Why on earth would a clown make a big deal about giving a child a rainbow-colored lollipop? Such a fuss should be reserved for something significant, something like pinning a medal on the lapel of a hero. Why would a lucratively employed medical doctor move his practice to the African bush and apply his skills to pygmies who had not asked for help and who would never be able to pay for treatment? What kind of value system is at work here? And what kind of clown is that person who prays about decisions instead of merely calculating the pros and the cons of various responses?

Not in a book on clowns, but in a volume on what it means to be a Christian, Hans Küng writes of the great reversal in values that accompanies a commitment of faith.[10] Commonly accepted priorities are radically reordered. What matters most to a majority of people may matter little to disciples of Christ. Even righteousness itself, as popularly perceived, may appear turned upside down.

Paradox is prominent among clowns as well as present at the heart of the gospel. Enid Welsford recorded a widely held perception of clowns when he wrote that a fool, a clown, "is an amphibian equally at home in the world of reality and the world of imagination."[11]

Numerous New Testament writers describe Christians as persons who are in the world but not of it—citizens of heaven who are colonized on Earth. Persons who believe the gospel live with paradox—as clowns, at home on that edge of existence where promise is becoming fulfillment and where the Kingdom of God is arriving amid the empires of this world.

Clowns are witnesses to truth and appreciate great simplicity. In the Hans Christian Anderson story entitled "The Emperor's Clothes," two swindling scoundrels had convinced the emperor they were outfitting him with a new suit of clothes that would be visible only to persons who possessed wisdom and the ability to do his job. When the emperor and his high officers viewed the new clothes, they saw nothing.

Of course they could not see anything because nothing was there. But no one wanted to admit stupidity and an inability to reign, so everyone complimented the beauty and magnificence of the tailors' work. The emperor then put on his invisible clothes and wore them in a royal procession.

Truth came from a child. Unintimidated by regal

expectations and cultural pressures, a child viewed the ridiculous sight. Unaffected by the fearful silence of the other spectators, she said, loudly enough for everyone to hear, "He has nothing on at all."

Clowns are childish in that they do not lose their simple innocence. A clown describes what he sees, speaks what he thinks, and expresses what he feels. Though initially some folks may react negatively to such blatant honesty, eventually most people realize that in a clown they meet somebody who in a miraculous way has "understood more life than we"[12] and is willing to share that understanding. Clowns tell it like it is. Pointing a finger at individuals and smiling from ear to ear, a clown calls an overweight person fat and an underweight person skinny. Irrational acts are dubbed stupid. Disinterested in disguise for the sake of society or compliance with conventional goodness, fears are screamed aloud, joys are danced, anger is vented, and grief is expressed by clowns. Disappointments are openly discussed and achievements are celebrated.

Invariably clowns threaten pretentious people and challenge the superficial. A clown can spot a fake at great distance. He sees what is wrong—he can see it every time—and says so. If personally involved in the wrong, he is disappointed and disgusted, if not ashamed. By nature, a clown wants things to be right. "He devalues by instinct, and his inverted vision is 20–20."[13]

From clowns we can learn not just to laugh but also to cry. From them too we learn when to laugh and when to cry as well as what to laugh or cry about. With their interest in simplicity, clowns bear witness to what is important and to what merely looks important, to what is only sensational and to what is truly fundamental. Because they have deep insight, typical tensions, worries, anxieties, and preoccupations annoy them less than they do most people.

Clowns never get far away from fundamentals. What clowns do that make them clowns are simple, predictable acts. In relation to faith, Henri J. M. Nouwen demonstrates great insight when he labels as "clowning around" such "foolish things as being alone, treasuring emptiness, standing naked before God, and simply seeing things for what they are."[14]

Simply stated, clowns are persons of integrity—as are Christians, of course. Was Jesus nurturing Christians or shaping clowns when he taught, "Let what you say be simply 'Yes' or 'No'" (Matt. 5:37)? Certainly clownishness is akin to faithfulness or vice versa. And faith is born out of integrity.

An integral reationship exists between the simple act of truth telling and the basic image of clowning—immediate and eternal. Morris West in his compelling novel *The Clowns of God* gives us this profound comment by his priest-character: "I became a priest to preach the word, to tell the good news of salvation. That's not something I can be prudent about, or safe, or even kind! And I have to give you the same message as I preach to the rest of the world. The battle between good and evil is already joined; but the good man looks like a fool, while evil wears a wise man's face and justifies murder by impeccable statistics."[15]

Clowns are liberated individuals who cling to an indefatigable hope. Another character in the West novel is a defrocked pope who is about to embark upon a critical mission. Having shared with a friend part of his strategy for world salvation, the former pontiff is told, "It sounds a little clownish to me." Undeterred by that judgment, the central character of the story, Jean Marie Barette, expresses excitement and declares his intention: "Then let's go the whole way! Let's admit that there is such a thing as divine folly. I'll sign myself 'Jeannot le Bouffon! Johnny the Clown.' "[16]

Once that decision was made and announced, Jean Marie found himself set free. People around him no longer could intimidate or discourage him. The clown label had freed him. Total liberty came with Jean Marie's new identity.

Freedom is a product of almost any combination of clown characteristics. To love vulnerably, to share unselfishly, to dream courageously, to know surprise intimately, to live on the boundary, and to appreciate simplicity are to experience liberty.

Witness a tall, gangling, big-nosed clown moving down an avenue in a parade, wandering where he wills. At times he mimics the precision of a marching band as he weaves between its columns, teasing the trumpeters, dodging the flying batons of the drummers, skipping around a sidewalk to test the patience of a police officer who serves as a parade marshal. At other times he mingles with onlookers in order to sit in the lap of an elderly woman, to share a teenager's popcorn, and to kiss a little girl. This man— this clown—is *in* the parade but not confined to the parade. With no compromise of character whatsoever, he can sit, ride, walk, or run where and when he desires.

For parade clowns freedom may be merely a matter of greasepaint and comic garb. For other persons the issue is a far more profound one, involving gift, redemption, character, and destiny. One theologian observes that to be in the world but not of it is to experience life without anxiety and thus with liberty.[17] Actually freedom is the cause as well as the consequence of such a life. The New Testament explains it best: "So if the Son makes you free, you are really free" (John 8:36).

A realization of freedom renders inconsequential life-stifling threats. Criticism is robbed of its capacity to intimidate and manipulate. Compassion can find unhindered expression apart from any fear about how it will be judged by other people. Unparalleled helpfulness is possible because liberated people can participate fearlessly and fully in the sufferings as well as the successes of those whom they love. Hope is indefatigable.

Even physical bondage and bodily punishment are deprived of any ultimate power by spiritual freedom. Take, for example, some of the pathetic yet majestic prisoners of World War II and Vietnam. Talk about clowns! Under the worst conditions possible these people laughed. Of course it was foolish. They were entombed by barbed wire lined walls, herded about by armed guards, humiliated daily—yet they laughed regularly. No number of affronts to their dignity or assaults on their integrity could succeed as long as they could smile—inwardly or outwardly. Laughter was a symptom of life's most basic kind of liberation. After all, hope is best known in a person's ability to laugh at hopelessness. These folks lived by laughing and hoping.

Though the reality of death is not destroyed, the threat of death is removed for a clown. Freedom to laugh in the present means that there is the possibility of laughter in the future, the promise of laughter in the life beyond. Read the taunt of the clownish apostle from Tarsus, who had discovered a kind of freedom and a quality of life that made death powerless "O death, where is thy victory? O death, where is thy sting?" (1 Cor. 15:15).

Is that mere fancy—an ideology to be desired but never achieved? By no means! A perception of the clownish nature of Jesus emerged earliest among his followers who were driven underground for safety. Etched onto the walls of the Roman catacombs was evidence that among these persecuted Christians "a new iconography" of Christ had developed. Slaves and derelicts for the most part, these believers realized the audacity of their faith and the ludicrous as well as dangerous nature of their position in society. It is little wonder that those early Christians envisioned and depicted Jesus as a clown and understood themselves to be fools for his sake. With this realization came a freedom that could not be altered. No longer were they threatened by anything. Listen to the words that were sung by members of this primitive community of faith as they were paraded to the Colosseum for execution: "We have lived and we have loved, and we shall live and we shall love again. Hallelujah!" Hallelujah? Yes, hallelujah. Imagine that!

On the movie screen Charlie Chaplin, more than any other person, epitomized a true clown. Invariably this tiny, mustached character was victimized by adversaries and ruthlessly buffeted about by others. Yet by the end of each episode, he was on his feet. The little man typically with his oversized shoes and with his big stick prominently displayed, shuffled his way down a road that led to a desert. Viewers were well aware that the road became smaller and smaller, but, *but!* the desert was there in the light.

Many a person, at one time or another, has played at

being a clown. But true clowning is not the same as playing. Along with the attractive aspects of clowning—freedom, vision, laughter, hope—goes the high cost of an uncommon dedication to clowning. To be a clown is not merely to do a foolish trick, but to model life conscientiously—life as intended in creation, life as made possible in redemption. Clown traits tend to develop in authentic discipleship.

A careful look at those clowns whose acts enliven the entertainment arenas of the world and whose images are splashed across the canvases of noted artists reveals the close similarity between these greasepainted characters dressed in comic garb and that thoroughly exemplary character produced by the gospel. There's little wonder that the fool label fits so well—that the clown name sticks to Christians. From the perspectives of both Scripture and culture, the gospel shapes clowns. These foolish figures show up everywhere the gospel is embraced, shared, and lived.

Look for the gospel and you will likely find some clowns. Do not be too surprised if you also discover history altered and life enhanced.

Martin Luther might just as well have had paint on his face and balloons in his hands at Worms. This little-known monk from Wittenberg took on the entire Roman Catholic hierarchy just because of a truth—*sola fide*—salvation by faith alone—he passionately believed to be true. "Here I stand," he said. But what some saw as courageous faithfulness, others viewed as incredible foolishness. Luther acted like a clown.

George Whitefield boarded a boat for the American colonies believing that the proclamation of the gospel of Christ could alter the spiritual course of the people on this continent. Just think, this bold fool embarked upon his monumental mission without the prospect of a television ministry!

Thomas More should have worn a rainbow-colored, funnel-shaped dunce's cap with a bright red ball on top. How else can you explain a respected member of the clergy and a counselor of nobility allowing himself to waste away in the Tower of London and ultimately losing his head in an execution because integrity was more important to him than life itself? What a clown!

Rosa Parks did not believe that she should have to sit in the back of a bus simply because her skin was black. Somehow she came to the ridiculous conclusion that God had made her in his image and had endowed her with a dignity and worth equal to that of any other person— black or white. Civil authorities rushed around Montgomery, Alabama, trying to get Parks back into her proper place just as net-carrying rescuers scamper about a circus tent trying to catch some crazy clown who has allowed herself to be launched into the air by a shot from a painted cannon.

It is reported that Emily Dickinson counseled a friend, "Be sure to live in vain, dear. I wish I had." Here was a strong suggestion that meaningful actions might not be measurable by popular standards. From this poet came encouragement that life be experienced at a level vastly different from that experienced by those people who play everything close to the vest, calculate each decision in relation to social opinion, and refuse ever to venture beyond boundaries prescribed by the majority. Live as a clown!

All of this sounds so very much like the counsel of the Christian gospel. Little wonder, really. Gospel truths shape these kinds of positive, influential personalities. Let's review the fundamental wisdom of the gospel: live in love even if treated with hatred, forgive when wronged, refuse to conform to the pressures of peers, keep the faith amid lures to doubt, be of good cheer even when things go bad, cling to joy despite collisions with troubles, live as light even when threatened by darkness. Both clowns and Christians are dedicated to a life that is abundant.

Clowns are alive and well everywhere the gospel is present and strong. The two go together. The gospel shapes clowns. So, today, look around. Where are the clowns?

4.   The World Needs Them

We have to have clowns. We just have to! All of us. Just as surely as God calls clowns and the gospel shapes clowns, the world needs clowns.

Actually, appreciation for clowns has a rather rough-and-tumble history. In one age the funny-faced facilitators of folly were considered emissaries from God, and in another time they were seen suspiciously as adversaries for evil. Sometimes appreciated as provocateurs of much-needed laughter, at other times clowns have been scorned as agents of irrelevance and disorder. Because public opinions have influenced stage presentations, there have been times when clowns were written into every script, even as there have been other times when they were banned from the stage.

Typically, ages of supposed enlightenment have not provided a climate conducive to acceptance of clowns. That is understandable. Viewed from the perspective of sophisticated reason, the playfulness of clowns is irrational, their attire is inappropriate, and their concerns are illogical.

In recent years a recognition of the clown's importance has resurfaced. At our best moments, and perhaps at our worst moments as well, we know that we need clowns in our lives. Look around and you can witness the reemergence of these devotees of delight—in drama, in literature, and even in works of art. But that is not the whole story.

At the present time, attitudes toward clowns are quite mixed. The heads and hearts of people are engaged in a tug-of-war as an attempt is made to decide which is more important. Clowns are lauded as characters of inestimable worth among those persons for whom the main concerns in life are joy, faith, peace, love, and appropriate expressions of the spirit. Appreciation for clowns is minimal, however, where the agenda for life is success measured by compliance with conventional logic, which assures cultural approval, and advancement in institutional structures, which guarantees the achievement of a lofty social status.

Nowhere is the radical ambivalence of people's reaction to clowns more apparent than in a discussion of society's need for them. Even those people who usually disregard the realm of the spirit occasionally appreciate the antics of clowns. For the most part theirs is a world of work amid Wall Street ticker tapes on investments, computer printouts of marketing accomplishments, and administrative charts that designate power. Yet these entrepreneurs of the business bureaucracy seem to sense the significance of people who exist without all of that—persons who know how to play.

Similarly, even the harshest critics of a gospel-infused life may eventually admit the necessity of faith because it benefits society. Many people fluctuate between affirming clowns in moments of elation and then seeking to devalue them by businesslike rationalizations. They desire the presence of clowns in pursuit of pleasure but suddenly become uncomfortable with them when faced with the prospect of being with them all the time. There is something in most of us that wants to emulate clowns so as to experience the joy of their liberation and the satisfaction of their contributions to life. But then in our more sober moments we are nervously excusing such aspirations as expressions of the immature inner child who is attempting to avoid the stress of the real world.

Maybe the paradox has been resolved best in the Zunis' attitude toward the Koyemci clowns in their communities. Among the people of this culture, clowns are considered to be silly but wise—both simpletons and sages. Though folks laugh at them, they also listen to their oracles and treat them as high priests and priestesses.

To be sure, the wisdom of God often appears to be folly when judged by the standards of this world. Conversely, the brightest reasoning of society is viewed as insanity by members of the community of faith. Anyone can predict the subsequent dilemma. Citizens of the Kingdom of God come off looking like fools, like clowns, to persons whose loyalties do not transcend the kingdoms of this world.

Except for the few rare occasions on which efforts have been made to rid the world of clowns completely, people generally have chosen to coexist with them— passively and uncomfortably or gratefully and compassionately. How different recorded history would be if this were not the case! Yes, the world needs clowns. In retrospect, gratitude to God is the most appropriate way to recognize those clowns who have preceded us. In prospect, a request to God for more clowns is the most responsible prayer for the days to come.

Reasons for our need for clowns are as many, as

various as the contributions that clowns can make to our lives. We have to have clowns.

Exemplars of Humanity

It has been wisely said that clowns make the circus human.[1] Wishful thinking aside, most people in a circus audience cannot identify with the gaudily dressed trapeze artists, the courageous animal trainer, or the ambidextrous jugglers. The clowns, though, are different. They are the ones to whom everyone's attention is drawn magnetically. Most people can identify with the clowns. They are like us. But not exactly.

Frederick Patka correctly recognizes the potential to be a clown as an essential component in the human personality. Every person can claim the possibility of this privilege because to be a human being "presupposes the possession of rational insight through which the comical and the tagical aspects of life can be perceived."[2]

Sadly, though, instead of living up to this wonderful, divinely given potential for clownishness, many people settle for much less and defensively justify their compromise by using the word *clownishness* as a disparaging epithet. The word *clown* is a title hurled at individuals who do not live down to the norms of those reduced expectations.

Rather than growing into authentic personhood and living fulfilled as clowns, far too many people are willing merely to function in ways of life that are less than truly human. These deluded folks settle in and become comfortable in their roles and assume a studied condescension that criticizes all who live beyond them—snickering at the more spirited, teasing those who are more human, jeeringly calling them clowns.

Similar circumstances occur spiritually. From the perspective of the gospel, all persons are invited and encouraged to be "fools for Christ's sake": clowns. Yet only a few people actually become what everyone can and should be. Most people, in order to justify their own life-stifling compromises, call clowns those persons who grow into a true humanity and experience life-enhancing fulfillment. At stake is an attempt to redefine life's most basic values—to label the wise as foolish in the hope that the truly foolish will then seem wise, even if all of the evidence in Scripture and life is to the contrary.

Clowns make life more human. For that reason, if for no other, the world cannot do without them.

Clowns enable us to confess our contradictions and to recognize our true potential as human beings. Imagine two clowns: a woman in a colorful evening gown and a man in a dirt-splotched, patched-up tuxedo. As they stroll with mock dignity into the spotlight of a center ring and the watchful eyes of spectators focus on them, suddenly the man trips. Falling helplessly but fitfully, he pulls the woman down with him. Onlookers are laughing—maybe without realizing it.

No sooner do the two comic characters regain their feet, straighten their evening wear, and begin to dance than the woman steps on the man's foot slightly and then with flair trips him up completely. Now everyone in the bleachers is laughing heartily, acutely aware that the same things could happen to them. Here are their counterparts in the circus.

But there is more. Both clowns get up again, and

before the lights go out, before the episode is ended, these two strangely elegant people of the night dance together with a fluid dignity and grace.

Think about it. From clowns come the worst and the best in life, the gaudiest and the most beautiful, failures and successes. Everyone finds in clowns something with which to identify. And in that identification truth dawns: disappointment need not lead to resignation, failure at one moment does not negate the possibility of success at another moment. For clowns, potential remains intact despite the presence of problems, and contradictions are not indicators of a flawed personality—only of a true humanity.

A major reason that clowns command so much attention and evoke such soul-felt laughter is that emerging from the absurdities of their actions are accomplishments that fulfill the highest of human aspirations. Clowns know how to turn the tables in all situations, to challenge those who seem to be in charge, to upset the powerful, to alter apparently immovable structures, to take on all opponents, and to win with a grin. Eric Auerbach's statement about Cervantes's don Quixote actually describes all clowns: "Don Quixote preserves a natural dignity and superiority which his many miserable failures cannot harm. . . . He even develops and grows kinder and wiser as his madness persists."[3]

We need that. How comforting to see a clown get up spryly after being knocked down ruthlessly and to see ourselves in that clown. How encouraging to know that a clown won't allow laughter on the part of others stop her from her pursuits. We need these models of humanity.

Clowns encourage us to accept vulnerability as an integral ingredient in true humanity. No clown worth his salt measures the advisability of an action by asking himself, Will this make me too vulnerable? In fact, if a clown wasn't willing to be vulnerable, he would never do anything very beneficial.

Emotional vulnerability is a way of life. A clown is aware that people may misunderstand, but joy is expressed in shouts of happiness, excitement emerges in jumping up and down, and pain is not concealed by lip-biting repression but revealed in ear-splitting cries. No one has to wonder what a clown is feeling. A clown's emotions are there for everyone to see, to respond to them or to attempt to take advantage of them. To be emotional is to be vulnerable.

Also, physical vulnerability is an ever-present reality for a clown. Only because a clown is willing to take a harsh spill and endure the subsequent bruises does she run at breakneck speed along a parade route or allow herself to be launched from a springboard and hurled from one side of an arena to the other. A rodeo clown is ineffective unless he accepts the dangerous possibilities involved in the process of distracting an angered, rampaging animal from the cowboy it has just thrown into the dirt.

Intellectual vulnerability is a necessity too. The desire to prompt a smile on the face of a troubled child or to give pleasure to a jaded invalid may require forms of behavior that detached observers consider crazy. Intentional acts of foolishness leave a person very vulnerable, but the child may laugh and the bedridden woman may know a moment of joy. Foolishness? If so, that's all right.

Relational vulnerability is often the most obvious

vulnerability of a clown. Frequently an excited clown reaches out to a beleaguered colleague, knowing full well that rejection is as much a possibility as acceptance. Among the most touching of antics performed by a clown are those where an interplay occurs between loneliness and fellowship, rebuff and welcome, criticism and affirmation. A tramp clown looks lovingly at a beautiful spectator and rolls his eyes, begging for recognition, knowing all the while that she will likely ignore him completely while others laugh at him.

Current estimates of maturity reflect a tragic erosion of an accurate understanding of humanity. Growth toward adulthood is equated with repressing sentiments, dulling sensitivities, taking charge, exercising control, and allowing no one "to get to you." How different from clowns. How inconsistent with a gospel that asserts that only as people become like children—sensitive, not in control—can they experience true life and inherit the Kingdom of God.

Devoid of vulnerability, a person's existence can be relatively safe but only remotely human. Over against a culture that counsels passivity and rewards mediocrity, both clowns and the gospel commend the vulnerability of a true humanity. We need clowns. They can soften our spirits, crack the crusty shells of our pseudosophistication, open our hearts, and raise our self-erected barriers of protection, making us more human.

Tragically, people who steel themselves against the possibility of vulnerability lose their humanity. Unless a person is willing to be abused, he or she is not likely ever to be of much use. Anything that protects vulnerability destroys humanity. Clowns know it and will not let it happen to them. That is another reason why the world so badly needs them.

Clowns expand the limits of our consciousness so that we can know the kind of honest humility that makes possible salvation and true righteousness. In the past Greek and Russian Orthodox churches observed the "holy fool" tradition. Periodically monks assumed the role of fools and engaged in strange, even bizarre, behavior. The intent of such action was to cause people to see the folly of their lives and to confess their need for piety.

"Even the simplest clown manages by gesture and incident to explore the mythology of self."[4] Whether gathered in a cathedral for some modern version of the ancient Feast of Fools or congregated before the make-shift stage of some clown in a carnival, attention to jesters moves us to introspection. In a clown not only do we see failures, weaknesses, pretensions, and needs like those that we experience, we see them and laugh at them. But unless we recognized these traits in others, we might never acknowledge their existence in ourselves. Thankfully, though, we will eventually attempt to cope with the things we learn about ourselves while laughing in the give-and-take of daily living.

Human beings have needs. Clowns know that and make no effort to hide it or deny it. They know that it is useless to worry that a presence of needs may cause others to withhold love. Actually, confessing needs, admitting weaknesses, and dealing with failures are crucial to emotional maturity. Spiritually, salvation cannot come apart from a person's request for it and acceptance of it. Piety too is known only by those unafraid to confront their humanity. We need both, for both salvation and piety are intended to make us more human.

Lords and Ladies of Laughter

Think of clowning and sooner or later you will start laughing. The two simply go together: clowns and laughter. All of us need both.

Laughter has almost as many different sources as it has varieties of expression. Fear often prompts nervous laughter. Giggling at trivia is one means of dealing with trauma. A person may not understand a cartoon or see the humor in a joke, but because everyone else is laughing, he laughs—superficially.

Hypocritical laughter can stem from a desire for self-defense. Persons who seek to protect themselves from the perceptions of others will laugh as if all is well even if they are experiencing pain, physically or emotionally. In the absence of genuine happiness, a smile is faked, a laugh is forced. Patronizing criticism can produce laughter of condescension. People look down their noses at a person whose behavior doesn't match their norms, and they laugh at her, maybe even call her a clown. Such laughter is a dagger hurled at her heart.

Within the church, laughter is a most intriguing phenomenon. Something that isn't funny anywhere else can evoke laughter in a church. Possibly that is because in a setting of holiness people want to laugh but feel a pressure to be serious. Unfortunately, some church people have sold out to solemnity under the illusion that emotional severity has something to do with being religious.

Often laughter accompanies spiritual insight. When a

breakthrough in understanding occurs, people nod and smile or laugh. I have observed that may times when a speaker makes a direct accusation of wrongdoing, listeners tend to nudge each other, smile at each other, and even sometimes laugh quietly together, as if to say, That's right. That's the truth that we (or they) need to hear.

Surely the rollicking, "mad" professor in the movie *Mary Poppins* sang a confession that most people could share: "I love to laugh." In truth, not only do people enjoy laughter, people need laughter. Frequently in counseling sessions a troubled person will comment longingly, "I just want to laugh again" or "I cannot remember the last time I laughed."

Clowns attract laughter of different sorts. Professional clowns, whose aim is to be funny, provoke a laughter of pleasure: a delighted response to entertainment. Spiritual clowns, who seek only to be faithful, elicit a laughter of ridicule: a cynical comment on unusual behavior. Strangely, though, both kinds of clowns are needed: fools and fools for Christ's sake. This world needs ladies and lords of laughter. All of us need clowns.

Laughter is essential to good health. In recent years a flood of materials has emerged documenting the physiological benefits of laughter. Representative of this material is the highly acclaimed work of Norman Cousins, who wrote about his encounter with and ultimate victory over a critical illness. Cousins has explored the medical value of humor theoretically. More important, though, he has experienced personally the therapeutic value of laughter: "Ten minutes of genuine belly laughter had an anesthetic effect and would give me at least two hours of pain-free sleep."[5] Support for such an appreciation for laughter can be found in biblical, philosophical, and medical sources.

Such truth sets clowns in a different light, does it not? From the perspective of a dedicated clown, "authentic humor is an instrument of agape-love, which means to will the well-being of the other."[6] For those who have benefited from clownish actions, humor is a therapeutic tool in the healing process.

Laughter is a fundamental component of any loving relationship. Students of human interaction agree that deep and meaningful relating is virtually impossible without joy, a sense of humor, and laughter. Based upon a careful examination both of the history and the nature of friendship, Martin E. Marty concludes that the best advice that can be offered to people seeking to develop a circle of friends is, "Be sure some of you can laugh."[7]

No relationship exists as an exception to Marty's observation. Unfortunately, though, many people attempt to bond associations, to form friendships, and even to solidify families by slavishly trying to follow a set of rigid rules for relating that are documented as steps to success in interpersonal dealings. Underlying this behavior is the false assumption that relationships can be achieved, like checkbooks can be balanced, sales agreements negotiated, or travel routes planned. Not so! Eugene Kennedy is on target when he says that true friendship is "at once illogical and profoundly meaningful."[8]

Growing relationships invariably involve what some folks may consider frivolous and wasteful expenditures of time and energy, accompanied by foolish laughter. Look carefully at such couples or groups laughing together— laughing with each other, laughing at each other, laughing

in pleasure, laughing in planning, laughing about themselves, just laughing. They are becoming one—laughing
their ways into one way. Admittedly, the validity of such
observations is difficult to accept in an increasingly
computer-oriented culture in which everything must
make sense. "A dried-out actuary calculating cost-benefit
ratios would probably conclude that friendship is not an
efficient enterprise."[9]

Laughter nurtures within people the kind of love that
will not settle for less than a whole relationship. People
who can laugh know also how to touch, run, and shout.
Laughter helps the tough to become tender. Leo Buscaglia
relates a passage from Donna Swanson's *Mind Song* that
paints a literary picture that serves to haunt anyone who
seeks relationships only by reasoned calculations, togeth-
erness without humor. A longtime widowed mother
reflects on the rational manner of child rearing that she
practiced. Now she is lonely. She has children who visit,
pay their proper respects, chat, and remember. But she
needs to be touched, and more. Her regretful words
constitute a memorable warning: "God, why didn't we
raise the kids to be silly and affectionate as well as
dignified and proper."[10] We need ladies and lords of
laughter.

Laughter is an inspiration for, and an indication of, hope.
Longtime circus clown Emmett Kelly observes that few
showpeople are suicidal. Despite unhappiness, sickness,
and even tragedy, these traveling minstrels retain the gift
of laughter and seldom give up hope.[11] The phenomenon
that this professional clown observes among his peers he
projects as the primary product of his own pranks, the
greatest gift of his presence before others: to help

troubled people laugh themselves toward hope. "By laughing at me," he says, "they really laugh at themselves, and realizing that they have done this gives them a sort of spiritual second wind for going back into the battle."[12]

Christians have much the same relationship to laughter, hope, and ministry. It is ironic, but those spiritual clowns that secular society laughs at most are the very people who cause the world to live most happily and hopefully!

Laughter is important everywhere—not just with applause under the big top of a circus tent or with singing in the sanctuary of a church, but even coupled with anxiety in a hospital ward or associated with the tragedy of a concentration camp. Reflecting on his experiences as a prisoner of war in a Nazi compound, Victor Frankl says he came to equate mastery of the art of living with the development of a sense of humor. Without laughter, Frankl and his colleagues in misery who survived might well have died. Many of the prisoners developed the ability to survive by nurturing a capacity to laugh even in a time of terror. In their laughter was a subtle form of power and the presence of hope. Clowns? Sure. Pitiful clowns in a sense—those who could laugh while others were dying. But hopeful clowns as well—hopeful clowns conditioned by the saving grace of laughter.

Do not misunderstand. Laughter in the face of trouble need not be indicative of a devil-may-care or who-cares attitude. Just the opposite. Grady Nutt liked to say that "laughter is the hand of God on the shoulder of a troubled world." That is more akin to the truth of the matter. An ability to laugh even in a time of crisis springs from the understanding that God cares. From this reassuring realization of divine compassion comes resilient laughter, persistent hope.

Laughter is a dynamic dimension of personal faith. Knowing when to laugh, with whom to laugh, and at what to laugh are every bit as important as knowing how to laugh. Clowns are the world's best instructors in the art of laughter. But those things that clowns can teach us go far beyond the intellect. Faith is crucial. Believing and laughing are integrally related.

To laugh at some aspects of human existence indicates sickness: is nothing holy? Not to laugh at other phenomena represents ill health: is there no joy? Knowledge of the difference between these two is nurtured by faith. Clowns are aware of the critical line of demarcation. They know when to poke fun, to joke, and to laugh and when to back off from a situation, with no attempt at humor.

Redemption is the source of a joy that makes wise laughter most possible and the cause of commitments that evoke critical laughter from other people. The very people who point out life's incongruities for the sake of improvement are themselves considered out of order, out of line, and odd by the standards of conventional judgment. In attempting to commend to others that which is related to laughter but more important than laughter, Christians are made the butt of bad jokes and the objects of scornful laughter. Keep in mind that clowns cannot enable people to laugh apart from the possibility of being laughed at personally. Only if Christian believers are willing to be laughed at harshly can they live redemptive lives.

Laughing can be a liberating experience. Persons able to laugh heartily are capable of throwing off those things that bind them unnecessarily and prevent an authentic life. In such laughter and liberty, faith becomes a possibility. Noted theologian Reinhold Niebuhr wisely speaks of humor as a "prelude to faith" and calls laughter "the beginning of prayer."[13]

Faith reacts to faith with joy and laughter. Mythologically, laughter dominated Dante's heaven. Biblically, laughter is a reality for all eternity—a quality of the redeemed life in both the present and the future. Each time a new person embraces such life through conversion, all of heaven reverberates with joy.

Servants with Sensitivity

Life is more than laughing, though. Human existence and rich religious experience must embrace both comedy and tragedy, happiness and sadness, laughter and tears. To seek one without the other or to settle for one apart from the other is to attempt to segment that which cannot be divided, to accommodate an inauthentic way of life, and to opt for the perpetration of a lie.

Theorists debate which phenomenon has priority: tragedy or comedy. Although some see comedy as secondary—always a late or an after-the-fact or an in-spite-of-the-fact experience—others make humor primary. Regardless of which is put first, neither one can be cast aside. Both tragedy and comedy persist. Each must be integrated into the experience of true humanity. Each is related to faith with integrity.

Laughter and tears come from the same source. Only a person who knows happiness can know sadness, and vice versa. Neither emotion negates the other. Rather, each emotion is close to the other—all of the time.

Culture seeks to commend a contrary opinion by way of a coercive myth. At an early age a hurt child is told, "Be a big boy and don't cry," or "Act like mother's little woman and smile." Toughness is in. Weakness is out. "Look happy even if it kills you." The results of such ridiculous counsel are hypocrisy in relation to self and insensitivity to others.

Clowns will not kowtow to such counsel. Capable of bountiful laughs and wailful tears, clowns show up with sensitivity and thus embody a promise of servanthood. Clowns realize that all people need both to laugh and to cry, and they can help in either experience.

Did you ever watch Emmett Kelly, the professional clown's clown? At first glance Willie—Kelly's circus name—was a picture of pathos: thin-soled, knottily laced, worn out, oversized shoes; dark and dirty clothing that hung awkwardly in layers of wrinkles, tears, and patches and had frayed edges; baggy, sagging pants; a bulky, flapping, much too large coat; a sloppy mismatched tie clipped smugly to a tarnished shirt by a rough wooden clothespin; splintery hairs protruding from underneath a battered old derby.

Willie's face was utterly captivating: an orange-red bulbous nose; cheeks and chin darkened by face paint, leaving the impression that he was unshaven or dirty; lips and mouth whitened in a forlorn expression; eyes obviously lively but most often downcast, with a constant hint of tears. By Kelly's own assessment, Willie was a "forlorn and melancholy little hobo."[14] Pathos was the perception at first glance. Yet to see Willie was to experience joy. To watch him perform was to know laughter. The very presence of Emmett Kelly as Willie the clown communicated both pathos and pleasure. His face was mournful but his actions graceful. From others' problems came the incentive for his pranks. From the tears that trickled down his cheeks came the smiles that spread across the faces of his observers.

Nowhere else but in a clown can such a perfect blend of sensitivity be found—except, of course, in the content of the Christian gospel. Sensitivity is the essence of Christianity. Read the gospel story carefully, and you will encounter it eventually: uncontrollable laughter and irrepressible tears, a triumphal entry and a lowly exit, a horrendous crucifixion and a glorious resurrection.

Clearly Christianity embraces both hurt and happiness, pain and pleasure, frustration and fortitude, disappointment and delight. Amid affirmations of the priority of praise is a recognition of the reality of pathos. Shouts of elation do not deafen believers to quiet sighs of depression. Consciousness of humor does not promote obliviousness to hurt. And awareness of the power of the gospel is not divorced from a recognition of the powerless. Even those happy folks shouting hallelujahs recognize and empathize with those persons too sad to whisper, much less shout, anything.

Hymn writers are particularly perceptive poets. Phillip P. Bliss caught the sensitive servant nature of Jesus when he wrote the hymn entitled "Man of Sorrows, What a Name." "Man of sorrows" was the first comment about Christ, but certainly not the only one or the final one. Indeed, the Lord who wept was a person acquainted with grief. Look quickly, though, to the end of Bliss's work, a conclusion of exultation: "Hallelujah, what a Savior!" The apparently contradictory expressions are actually of one piece. To understand Jesus correctly requires a recognition of both of these aspects of his personhood. Christ

could be the one—either one—because he was the other.
Man of sorrows. Source of hallelujah. What a Savior!

True followers of Christ display the same sensitivity
that their Master does. Again a piece of music makes the
point precisely. A well-known old spiritual begins with
the confession, "Nobody knows the troubles I've seen,"
continues with "nobody knows the sorrow," and concludes with "glory, hallelujah." Neither depression nor
elation can be denied or ignored. Attempts to sublimate
one in order to exalt the other result in a loss of faith.
Sensitivity involves the capacity to laugh and to cry. A
cross in the heart does not remove a hallelujah from the
lips. As Walter Kerr writes, "To be funny is to have been
where agony was."[15]

"Are you laughing or crying?" Such a question is
apropos for clowns and for Christians. Both smiles and
sobs are a part of faith and of sensitivity. Each nurtures a
greater capacity for the other. At points we laugh about
what is and weep over its shortfall in relation to what
could be. Then again, we cry over what is and, buoyed by
a vision of promise, laugh at what is possible. Smiles and
tears are never very far apart.

This world desperately needs sensitive souls—servants
with sensitivity. That is why clowns are so important, and
Christians. Fools for Christ's sake know how to laugh but
refrain from total hilarity because of their acquaintance
with tragedy. Joy is exuded but sorrow is not ignored.

Clowns, step forth! Where darkness is real, someone
needs to strike a match, light a candle, point the way to
light, or live as light. Where death is an ominous reality
and a constant threat, folks are needed who can speak of
matters more important than death and display a quality
of life that death cannot destroy. Where diversity is a

source of detrimental division, persons are needed who can say a good word for unity, express affirmation, include all kinds of people in their fellowship, and conduct a chorus in which everyone can participate. Where the future appears to be closed, people need to step forth to knock out some windows, to construct some doorways, and to remind us of the unpredictable. Only those with authentic sensitivity and a penchant for servanthood can do it. Only clowns can be of much help.

Walter Kerr catches a vision of the importance of clowns. "What a good man the clown is," he writes, "to endure so much, to survive so relentlessly, to keep us company in all weathers, to provide us with a way of looking at the worst that enables us to take a temporary joy in the worst!"[16] Kerr's comments could apply equally well to Christians—with one exception. The joy provided by these clowns is permanent rather than transient, eternal rather than temporary.

We need clowns. The world must have some clowns. None of us can survive for long deprived of servants with sensitivity.

Facilitators of Festivity

When festivity fades from a culture, all of life is jeopardized. Individuals and institutions specifically are endangered, as are humanity and society generally.

Clowns are the best bet for guaranteeing an ongoing festivity. Instinctively a clown can cause a celebration in almost any situation and from those persons present evoke joyful participation. That is why historically in traditional festivals clowns were valued highly. Then clownish folly was not considered a behavioral defect but appreciated as a moral strength, a commendable quality that endeared the clown to the rest of the community.

Many students of modern society have expressed concern over the present lack of genuine festivity. In order to prevent this situation from becoming more critical, a broad-based rebirth of festivals is essential. The world needs clowns—those comical creatures who so adeptly facilitate festivity.

Development of a healthy humanity is partially dependent upon the presence of festivity. Festivals provide necessary insights into a person's significance in and relationship to time. Festive moments foster for sensitive persons a proper perspective on the past, the present, and the future. Festivity offers occasions for the events of immediate history to interact with the rhythms of eternity, thus freeing human spirits to soar ecstatically and feeding bountifully the innate hunger of human souls. In any age the quality of humanity is downgraded by a drought of festivity.

Realization of community requires cooperation in festivity. By no other means are neighbors, near and far, bound to each other so intimately in fellowship as when they share festivity as a group. Enthusiastic participation in meaningful celebrations results in a lowering of self-constructed and cultural guards; words are spoken joyfully, opinions are exchanged freely, and emotions are released honestly. Arm in arm, people laugh together— maybe even laugh until they cry. Or cry until they laugh. Relationships are established. Interdependence is encouraged. Society is solidified. Community is realized.

Festivals provide both the symbols of unity and the actual realization of community. Consequently periods of festivity protect a community as persons return to them again and again. No wonder that Harvey Cox observes, "Our survival as a species may depend in part on . . . authentically worldwide festivals, with their symbols of a single global community."[17]

Growth in spirituality necessitates personal participation in festivity. Frequently the most profound convictions of faith are discovered, embraced, and nurtured more in festive celebrations than in oratorical declarations, cerebral reflections, or solitary meditations. What people fail to grasp by means of traditional methods of teaching and preaching, they often see clearly and seize readily in celebrating. Likewise, what people believe deeply but cannot express verbally, they can sing, draw, or play.

After all, the truth of the Incarnation cannot be captured in words or conveyed by theological theories or philosophical principles alone. Festivals are needed. A season of Advent and the festivities of Christmas put people in touch with the reality of "God with us." Similar celebrations are required to commend the truth of resurrection and the invitation to conversion. Some beliefs simply must be sung, others danced, and still others behaved. Faith does not grow apart from festival times, which are attuned to the doubts and certainties, sorrows and joys, of the faithful.

Not surprisingly, Jesus of Nazareth understood the necessity of festivity. Jesus enjoyed fellowship meals with his disciples regularly and defended those happy experiences to critics who would have replaced feasting with fasting. Additionally, on numerous occasions he dined, talked, and laughed with members of society who were castigated by the religious establishment. Harsh labels were hurled at Jesus. Scoffers spread rumors that the preacher from Nazareth was a glutton, a drinker, a partyer: a clown. It is interesting, though, that when Jesus acknowledged these critical charges publicly, he related them to the results of God's wisdom (Matt. 11:19). From the perspective of a sick religion, even as from the point of view of a secular world, conformity to God's will inevitably results in behavior interpreted as the foolish festivity of clowns.

The itinerary of Jesus' social engagements does not tell the whole story, though. To many, declarations from Jesus were every bit as disturbing as his actions were. (Actually, both were terribly enlightening!) "I assure you that unless you change and become like children," he said, "you will never enter the Kingdom of God" (Matt. 18:3, translation mine). Imagine the responses evoked by that statement: "Now this is serious. How can he speak lightly about eternity? The very idea of relating childishness to citizenship in the Kingdom of God! Does he know the importance of moral casuistry? And what about the need to develop a systematic theology? What does a child have to do with the Kingdom of God?"

Jesus was discussing the importance of humility; he was discussing the importance of festivity as well. "Become like children," he said. Think about it.

From a child we can learn to celebrate—to celebrate simply and spontaneously. For children, festivities do not have to be planned far in advance and produced by extravagant economics. In fact, some of the most festive moments imaginable are not at all predictable. An act, a sight, or a sound evokes joy and excitement. One child shares the experience with others and all become caught up in it. A festival erupts on the spot, at that moment— laughing, talking, dancing, shouting, playing, and perhaps even a form of praying. Not a great deal is required to invite such action. A celebration of the wonders of creation, for example, can be prompted by no more than sighting an oddly shaped cloud, tasting the cold wetness of new-fallen snow, discovering the first daffodil of spring, finding a hiding frog, or hearing a bird singing.

Clowns have the same capacity for celebrations as do children and share an appreciation for the simplicity and spontaneity of them. Noticing the dancing eyes and smiling face of a small child watching a parade can cause several clowns to abandon their separate frolicking, come together, laughing as a group, and seize a serendipitous moment for celebrating.

Both clowns and children have an uncanny ability to chalk off space—geographically or psychologically—in any situation and give themselves to a celebration. Neither the immediate context nor the question of timing nor conventional expectations are allowed to be stifling. Remember that at the most somber moment in Jesus' ministry, in a setting fraught with crisis, he shared with his disciples an ancient meal characterized by festivity—the Passover—and initiated a new meal intended to be continued with joy—the Lord's Supper. Is this at least a partial explanation for Cox's designation of Jesus as "the man of sorrows in the foolscap?"[18]

Devoid of heralds of hilarity, life is deprived of festivity. A passivity that breeds mediocrity is passed off as maturity! How sad. Conditioned by cultural philosophies that attempt to pigeonhole every experience, program every emotion, and maintain coolness and calmness at all costs, people feel uncomfortable with festivals and allow laughter only within appropriate limits. Explosive, head-laid-back, heartfelt outbursts of laughter are replaced by studied little sounds that are enough like laughter to be respectable but not so much like laughter as to be noticeable.

Neither clowns nor children can live like that. Thank God! These celebrants of joy will not be intimidated by social norms that attempt to define acceptable expressions for their happiness. Such a pretentiousness compromises life and assures death—even if the dead still breathe and walk. Contrary to popular projections of sophistication and suspicions of immaturity, a capacity for hilarity is a mark of true wisdom and exemplary maturity. We need clowns.

Without the influence of students of spontaneity, life is characterized by stark rigidity. Everything must be scheduled. Consequently, serendipitous moments are missed and festive celebrations repressed because of "prior engagements." This familiar litany of expectations indicates our identification of inflexibility as an enviable strength: "I wanted to laugh out loud, but I was in a business meeting." "This calls for a celebration—just as soon as we can get to it." "I am simply too busy for a party."

Tragically, such an approach to life can rob a person of such superlative experiences as the thrill of turning aside from everything else to watch a child take her first steps and then throwing a party to celebrate the achievements, or canceling a day's appointments to attend the circus with a family member, or listen to an excited teenager tell about an honorary recognition he received. Slaves to schedules become deaf to the screams of sea gulls, blind to the beauty of sunsets, and dull to the lure of happy interruptions. A person must be able to abandon a plan or deviate from an intention in order to experience a celebration.

Children and clowns commend spontaneity by their words and deeds. Leo Buscaglia says it best: "We love clowns. For a time their behavior sets us free from the straightjacket of convention, the predictability of a routine life and expectations of behavior. They touch the deep desire within all of us to let go of inhibition and get in touch with our natural spontaneity, our natural madness."[19]

From children we also can learn how to play. For children, nothing is off limits in play. In fact, some of the most enjoyable games for youngsters involve serious concerns for adults: they play at activities related to weddings, funerals, work, worship, and family. An outdoor swimming hole becomes a baptistry, a closet is considered an office, a high limb on a tree is treated as the cockpit of an airplane, and a stool set up in front of a few scattered chairs serves as an amphitheater or a church sanctuary. Donning some old, out-of-style, too-large, castoff adult clothing gives credibility to their make-believe. Children play seriously and happily, at times even hilariously.

Clowns also play that way and teach us how to play. Watch them. Dressed in ridiculous garb, clowns play festively—mocking presidents of corporations, mimicking doting parents, or making fun of military personnel. No enterprise is too serious to escape clownish playfulness.

People incapable of play have nothing to do but work for the sake of work, competing—or fighting—with their peers, growing tired in their bodies and weary in their minds and sick in their souls. If playfulness is out, so is

festivity. Appointment-oriented, clock-governed schedules become the dominant factor in their life scripts.
Obligations to tasks are more important than relations
with people, devotions of the heart. Spirits grow dull. Joy
disappears.

"Unless you change and become like children . . . "
Jesus said. He could easily have said "like clowns." "Be a
clown!" Who could possibly dispute the world's need of
clowns.

Frederick Buechner affirms the value of festivity.
Perceptively he relates the play of children to the growth
of Christians: "Maybe what is good about religion is
playing that the Kingdom will come, until—in the joy of
your playing, the hope and rhythms and comradeship and
poignancy and mystery of it—you start to see that the
playing is the first-fruits of the Kingdom's coming and
God's presence within us and among us."[20]

How we need a reemergence of joy. What a contribution facilitators of joy could make to our world. Bring on
the clowns!

Critics of Society

In Winston Brebner's novel *Doubting Thomas,* the
major character is troubled by life in a high-technology
society. At a given time each year this man disguises
himself as a clown and mingles with people out in the
streets and in the stores. Reactions to him are mixed. Not
all goes well. Some people subject him to gross indigni-
ties, but he endures each of them with patience, grace,
and dignity.

Eventually, though, he becomes famous. Many people
actually thank him: "You have a special gift, Mr. Clown

. . . for making us laugh at ourselves, at our weaknesses, our foolish suspicions, our pretensions."[21] But eventually the tables turn completely. People who had earlier accepted and praised him turn against him. Finally the clown is persecuted unreasonably and in the end "hilariously crucified"[22]—killed by those who had loved him.

Brebner's work provides a striking parable of society's reactions to clowns. Whether from the perspective of professional clowns in pursuit of their art form or biblical clowns in faithfulness to their way of life, the story is pretty much the same. Love is a given—the clown loves the people and the people love the clown. At first people respond with laughter and appreciation to a clown's actions—even to his protest of their social situation. Eventually, however, the spectators turn on their entertainer, society reacts negatively to its comical potential redeemer. As a result the clown suffers at the hands of the very persons he loves, those to whom he tries to bring joy. Ironically, because of this suffering, society often awakens to a realization of its own cruelty and is thus helped.

William Willeford is correct in his conviction that "some fools . . . have a direct responsibility for the well-being of society."[23] For each one it is labor characterized by cost and filled with love.

Prophets of protest

Society needs to take a long, fresh look at those things at which clowns poke fun. Behind several of their funny stunts and crazy pranks are serious statements of protest. So often clowns look like prophets and prophets look like clowns.

Clowns instinctively challenge pretense and snicker at

status. Symbols of success are made the objects of jests. A beleaguered but cocky clown strolls across the floor wearing a mock business suit of uncoordinated fabrics and riotous colors. He is carrying a beat-up attaché case covered with gaudy travel stickers and cracked open just enough to be strewing all kinds of papers. He is trying so hard to convey dignity that immediately he prompts hilarity.

Off in a corner another clown is seeking to emulate an appearance-minded golfer. He is garbed in a "sporty golfing outfit" of dirty tennis shoes, plaid knee socks, blimp-like cutoff pants, a multicolored sweater, huge, wide-rimmed sunglasses, and a bent out of shape hat. In his hands is a short-shafted, large-headed club that he swings, with exaggerated aplomb, at a tiny ball set atop an oversized tee.

Humorously aware of the intensely businesslike demeanor of the one clown and of the studied playfulness of the other, onlookers become a little uneasy with caricatures that too closely resemble reality.

Clowns reject a rigidly defined status within a tightly structured society. They jokingly flaunt a disregard for expectations of conformity.

Imagine a band of clowns mimicking a meeting of the board. Feigning the highly stylized behavior of business executives, the clowns are funny—suggesting campaigns, arguing their cases, and making motions.

Laughter accompanies the antics of clowns imitating social gatherings, such as receptions or banquets. Their exaggerated compliance with etiquette evokes smiles and a reexamination of the rules of politeness. Remember that clowns dress poorly not because they have to, but because they want to. Even stylish wear is tarnished intentionally or worn inappropriately. Effort is exerted to see that the emphasis is on persons—not on structures, fashions, traditions, expectations, status, or the like.

Clowns are unintimidated by crowns. Queens and kings, premiers and presidents, are people too. Everyone in a society is benefited when that fact is remembered, and clowns attempt to make it difficult to forget. Any vanity among officials is exposed as immaturity. Neither in the ring of a circus nor in the tetrarch's house in Jerusalem, neither in a street parade nor at the Diet of Worms, neither on the stage of a theater nor in the oval office of the White House, has there ever been a human being elevated to a position beyond question or above criticism. In fact, clowns revel in poking fun at people in prestigious places.

Clowns call into question misplaced priorities within society. Persons who measure every action by the predictable expectations of peers, come off looking like stiff-necked, wooden-hearted puppets manipulated on dangling strings held by the "dress for success" authorities. To be sure, a case can be made that clowns overreact to public pressures and the status quo. Clowns will go to almost any length to assure that no aspect of human society, or society itself, is regarded as an absolute.

In Morris West's *Clowns of God,* a fictitious character about to embark on a serious mission is in need of financial support. A concerned friend offers instructions on how a bank loan should be requested. Proper dress and appropriate behavior are stressed. The novelist displays wisdom in the words that are the response of the man in need: "I have little time and much travel to do. I will not be inhibited by the bureaucratic nonsense of your bank."[24] A prophet of protest? A true clown!

Must a man wear a three-piece business suit with a striped tie in order to voice a need respectably or to respond to a need helpfully? Look at a shabby clown who evokes sympathy and commends joy. Does a woman have to be wealthy in order to contribute significantly to society? Watch a clown who reeks of poverty seize a wonderful opportunity successfully. Can happiness come only when planned for extravagantly, with every aspect of life ordered perfectly? Do not believe it for one moment. Recall how in the antics of clowns, joyful redemption comes out of total chaos. Is an action beneficial only if it meets with social approval? The truth of that matter is dramatized by those devotees of delight who display love and do good deeds in a manner that pseudo-sophisticates consider ludicrous.

Advocates of authenticity—that is who they are. Thus protest is inevitable. Count on it. Clowns will kick and scream before every attempt to reduce life to a monologue, or to make it mere conformity to some book of rules. They know better. Clowns understand that life is poetic—filled with surprising initiatives, caring dialogue, and exciting rhythms of the spirit. Unless her study is done humorously to protest a lack of authenticity, you will not find a clown poring over a volume of guidelines or assessing possible public reactions before acting to express love or moving to demonstrate devotion.

Clowns occasionally qualify as rebels but usually not as revolutionaries. Clowns are not reformers by intention. Though clowns may dramatize the need for improvements and renovations, rarely do they demand radical innovations.

Typically judgments from clowns are inferred rather than screamed. Prophecy is subtle. Prods are gentle.

Causing trouble is a foreign thought to clowns. Enhancing life, encouraging joy, and prodding fulfillment are their goals.

Periodically someone such as Martin Luther sets in motion a movement that takes unforeseen and never-intended directions. More good results from such a cause than the initiator ever envisioned. Offended or frightened critics cry, "Clowns!" Informed historians are wiser and kinder. It is usually only in retrospect that such an influential individual is recognized as a reformer.

For clowns, wealth is much more of a qualitative matter than a quantitative concern. Richness is defined not by an accumulation of goods but by expressions of good.

Of course society does not understand. Two characters—both believable though fictional—make the point. A father, embarrassed by the fact that his son is a clown, explains his unwillingness to provide parental support. He says that "he couldn't give his money to a clown who would do only one thing with it; spend it, the very opposite of what you were supposed to do with money."[25] When the son is asked, "What kind of man are you?," he replies, "I am a clown—and I collect moments."[26] Moments! Of such is clownish wealth: meaningful moments, unique experiences, loving relations, vistas of beauty.

Wanted or not, clowns are needed. Clownish protests point to a cherished promise—the promise that life can be better, more than it is. Clowns are a vital link to light— light that places in proper perspective true priorities and worthy agendas. By way of their humorous antics, clowns make serious points. Cynicism, pretense, mechanism, superficial status, and moral relativity are challenged in order that hope, authenticity, personalism, human dignity, and primal moral values can be commended.

Proponents of love

True prophets really care for the people among whom they register protests. In fact, compassion for people is the source of their desire for changes in society. Clowns comply with this general principle. Clowns are deeply affectionate social critics. Hatred, bitterness, and vindictiveness have no place in their performance.

Humor is an effective instrument of social change that clowns know how to handle with great skill. Though a clown may prompt an audience to look at a common cultural quirk in their behavior or a moral aberration in their society, the ultimate strategy is to focus laughter on himself. Only after having laughed at the clown are people likely to laugh at themselves and their situations. Thus protests are registered empathically and nudges toward changes are offered gently.

Negatives are the servants of positives for clowns, and laughter is "the spoonful of sugar" that makes the negatives "go down." Judgment is never offered for the sake of judgment. Rather, judgment is employed in the interest of betterment. A no is shouted or a protest dramatized in order that a yes can be declared and an affirmation emphasized. One form of behavior is criticized in order that a higher and better form of behavior can be endorsed.

Laughter prompted by clowns is a provision for positive engagement with problems, not an avenue to detachment from them. Comic comments about present undesirable situations are intended as an invitation, with encouragement to a search for significant change. Mechanization is derided in order that fulfillment can be pursued. Antics that pan the senselessness of violence are meant to highlight the attractiveness of peace. Social status as the source of personal importance is subjected to severe scorn in order that individual dignity can be seen as a fundamental trait of every member of humanity. Poverty paraded humorously provides a backdrop against which a point about the importance of sharing can be made dramatically.

As critics of society clowns are proponents of love— lovers who will and work for that which is best for those whom they love. The actions of clowns can be correctly deemed a "caress of life."[27]

Brunts of punishment

Ironically, more often than not, people who labor for a better society end up getting hurt by the very people they seek to help. And clowns have the bruised bodies, injured spirits, and fractured hearts to establish this truth.

People do not like protest even when it is registered in love. Critical comments about the present that awaken an awareness to the possibility of needed changes do not fare well in the marketplace even when they are conveyed with gentle humor. Good times can turn bad quickly. Audiences who had cherished Charlie Chaplin and laughed at his every move turned in another direction immediately and complained bitterly when the funny little man's character commented on the wrongs of modern times.

The very sensitivity that prods a clown toward social protest positions her to get hurt. In a genuine effort to establish the dignity of every person, the dignity of the clown is injured. Unfortunately most people do not even know what has happened. Laughingly they view indications of the injury as just another dimension of the clown's comic routine.

All too often the greatest contributors to life are the ones who suffer most profoundly. Those who intend to help people laugh happily and change beneficially are often punished for their efforts. True to the nature of clowns, though, they attempt to wring some good even out of bad developments. Negative reactions from society are endured patiently as a further form of protest against society and as another indication of love for society.

Even when punished, the prophets remain lovers. The clowns! What on earth would we do without them?

Authors of Liberty

Who in the world is as free as a clown? Or as filled with fun? Physical boundaries fail to confine him. Social expectations do not restrict him. Mental categories cannot contain him. Thus the realm of the possible is redefined regularly and the promise of the future expanded considerably. Both are enjoyable.

Orations on freedom are unnecessary. The very identity of a clown is one of liberty. Actions speak for themselves. Not even the most basic rules of convention appear applicable to a clown's intentions. Gravity is defined as a motorized bug-shaped car suddenly starts up the side of a wall. Vision is baffled as a giant clown instantaneously is reduced to midget size or made to disappear. Normal patterns of cause and effect are disrupted. Hurt is inflicted by one clown on another, but laughter erupts when pain is predictable.

Clowns really are something special in relation to

freedom. Frequently observers cannot tell if they are working or playing, meticulously carrying out an assignment or merely seeking enjoyment. If the play of clowns is work, no one but the clowns know it. Each of their activities appears as an expression of liberty.

A short little fellow, noticeable only because of a bright red-and-chartreuse bow tie larger than his head, drives a jeep helter-skelter, in no apparent pattern. Whether actually following a charted course or simply turning at random, his piloting speaks freedom.

A stout woman with her bushy blonde hair pulled up in curls and wearing a much too large man's tuxedo teeters atop a tiny platform, hilariously grabbing at a swinging trapeze. Whether foolish frivolity or skillful artistry, the scene communicates liberty. So often spectators cannot distinguish between risks and rituals, innovations and repeat performances, or laughing and crying when clowns are involved. These fun-filled characters are free for either or for neither. Clowns are free.

Actually, humor and freedom are integrally related. Laughing and liberating go together—laughing that is liberating, laughing while liberating, laughing as a result of liberation. Good humorists and effective liberationists share much in common. Little wonder then that the identity of clowns and one of the prime ways in which they benefit society is as authors of liberty.

Of course not all clowns are in circuses, just as not all clowns wear painted faces and funny clothes. Often the title of clown is hurled as a term of derision rather than assumed as the name of a noble profession. From the perspective of culture, many people with a passion for liberation appear to be little more than fool-hearted clowns. M. Conrad Hyers recognizes and describes this type of person: "not the clown as self-styled buffoon but the person labeled by others as a clown, one who by his 'divine madness' gives expression to the special freedom that he has attained, and who in that freedom reveals some truth . . . or in some bizarre way becomes the agent of redemption in a particular situation."[28]

Clowns are liberated people—free from convention, expectation, regulation, and maybe even pain. Not only do clowns incarnate freedom, they also invite it and encourage it. The liberated are liberators. As they cavort, laugh, talk, and play, clowns provide a different point of view of life for many people. New insights into truth, beauty, value and joy are discovered. Observers want to know in a personal way what they see in clowns, and clowns inspire the courage to attempt such knowledge. So the freedom of clowns becomes freeing for others.

Risk is involved. But when it is accompanied by laughter, so what?

A popular author declares "A life devoid of mystery and risk is only half a life."[29] True. But more is involved than a single life. Liberty makes possible the kind of risk that makes liberty possible. Constant conformity to convention can lead only to captivity. An absolute necessity for broad-based social experiences of liberty are individuals already free enough to risk ventures into mystery. That is why laughter is so important.

Often laughing is what precipitates liberating. Laughter among people who are free generates concern for people who are not free. A good sense of humor among liberators serves as an antidote to predictable fears caused by the inevitable barriers to, and dangers of, liberation. Laughs of freedom and the freedom to laugh produce people who go about laughing while freeing.

Sydney Smith, who died in 1845, was a member of the Anglican clergy. To this man's credit were actions that caused the British Parliament to grant permission for Roman Catholics to vote in British elections. Additionally, Smith prepared the way for Parliament to approve the abolition of slavery. One observer concludes that Sydney Smith did more than any other person in history "to prepare the background of the emancipation of American slaves, the Russian serfs, and the slaves of Brazil."[30] The same writer also comments that Smith was "about the funniest person who ever lived."[31] Nor surprising, really.

Of course liberation agendas include more than freeing individuals alone. Sometimes whole societies are the enslaved. Prevailing mentalities can be the captors. Breaking certain kinds of bondage may call for an attempt at innovation that requires the kind of risk prompted by laughter and exemplified by clowns.

An old motto from the British War Resisters League is apropos: "It is madness to sail a sea that has never been sailed before; to look for a land, the existence of which is a question. If Columbus had reflected thus he never would have weighed anchor; but with this madness he discovered a new world."[32] Hear! Hear! Where would this world be were it not for those risk-taking clowns—either clowns by chosen profession or by self-designation or by castigation—who acted on their beliefs that illnesses could be cured, machines could fly, slaves could be freed, and life could be improved!

Clowns free up a crowd—even as they do an individual, an institution, or a society. Often their instruments of liberation appear impractical at best, foolish at worst: a fuzzy little dog, a monkey on the back of a pony, a tiny baby buggy, a weird wardrobe, or an enduring love, a disciplined nonviolence, a reconciling forgiveness, a peace with justice. When people are set to laughing, though, inhibitions weaken, fears fade, happiness prevails, and new adventures can be chosen.

Hope resides in such risk. Hope is born amid efforts aimed at liberation. Life can change. Tomorrow really can be better than today. Listen to the laughter—it is there at the beginning and at the end. Look for the clowns. Surely they will be around. We cannot do without them. Clowns are the proponents of risk and the harbingers of hope; they live among us as authors of freedom.

To the starving people of Calcutta, Mother Teresa may look like an angel—an angel of mercy. Honestly, though, to many other folks this little woman looks like and sounds like a clown—the epitome of irrationality. How out of step with society is her philosophy: "By having nothing we will be able to give everything—through the freedom of poverty."[33] Give everything! The freedom of poverty?

Why would any sane person choose to spend time, energy, and talents—to invest a life—among the terminally ill, serving sick and dying persons who in many instances cannot even say "thank you," much less pay in other ways for the assistance? When asked if this was not "rather a mad thing to do," one of Mother Teresa's colleagues in care, a member of the Sisters of the Missionaries of Charity, explained, "That is precisely why I came here—I wanted a very hard life. I wanted to be able to give up something."[34] What a clown! In fact, what clowns!

As long as he performed on concert stages, delivered lectures to university faculties, or practiced medicine in health care centers of Europe, Albert Schweitzer was heralded as a world-renowned genius. But when he moved his practice to the jungles of Lambarene, many dubbed him an international clown. Explaining that only a person who can find value in and devote himself to every kind of activity has the inner right to assume as his duty some extraordinary task rather than an actual or predictable one, Schweitzer observes: "Only a person who feels his preference to be a matter of course, not something out of the ordinary, and who has no thought of heroism, but just recognizes a duty undertaken with sober enthusiasm, is capable of becoming a spiritual adventurer such as the world needs. There are no heroes of action; only heroes of renunciation and suffering."[35] Albert Schweitzer, the clown!

On and on the record goes. Both big-name and no-name people populate any list of mad redeemers, mind-boggling clowns. Think, though, of where this world would be without such people. What an inestimable difference for good they have made in our lives!

We need clowns—people who can perform missions of mercy in unmerciful situations, people committed to peace amid violent revolutions, people willing to live for others while most others are seeking to live only for themselves. Clowns keep us in touch with our humanity, prod us into healthy laughter, sharpen the blunted edges of our sensitivity, facilitate expressions of genuine festivity, and involve us in both the blessings and the responsibilities of liberty. And in so doing they serve us with great integrity.

Emmett Kelly concludes his autobiography by reflecting on his need to stop reflecting in order to answer the ever-recurring call to clowning. Envisioning the arrival of that magic moment just prior to showtime, when everyone is in his or her proper place and waiting for the fanfare, Kelly observes, "There's a five-second period when the whole show seems to hold its breath. Now! The shrill blast of the whistle, the cornets and the cymbals and we're rolling. Come on, 'Willie'; here we go again."[36]

The world waits for clowns as if perpetually locked into that five-second gasp. We have to have some clowns. So where are they now, when we need them?

Dear God, let the drums roll, the whistles blast, the cornets blow, and the cymbals clash. We need some clowns. Send them to us, please. Where are the clowns?

5. The Church Encourages Them

Where are the clowns? I raise the question once more because clowns *have* needs as well as *meet* needs. After all, clowns are human—people who may be even more honest about their humanity than most. Disappointments distract them. Failures frustrate them. Clowns know all too well the realities of fatigued consciences, beleaguered convictions, wearied spirits, and discouraged souls.

Jesters stalking about on stilts cannot possibly perpetuate joviality through one parade after another without periodically dismounting for rest, refreshment, and replenishment. Not every second can be spent before spectators under the big top. Circus clowns must know moments out of the spotlight to look at themselves without greasepaint. Each one deserves to be a recipient as well as a dispenser of renewal. Rodeo clowns cannot interminably leap into rubber barrels, scale arena walls, and dodge charging bulls. Required are occasions for the recovery of courage and strength.

Clowns benefit from personally identifying each other and regularly getting together—and more. Someone has to make the clowns laugh. Someone has to give the clowns joy. Clowns must be made the beneficiaries of the same kind of life-enhancing sustenance that they so generously share with others. Clowns need encouragement.

While at a conference table at corporate headquarters, a businessperson struggles to do what is right as well as what is profitable, when profit seems to be all that is expected. Colleagues consistently counsel, "Lighten up. Don't be a fool. All we want is for you to assure us all of a hefty gain." That executive officer needs the reinforcement of like-minded people who declare, "We are with you. Stick to your convictions. Look like a fool if you must. Integrity is important."

A teenage girl has resolved to practice personal purity. Not unexpectedly, her popularity is at stake. She is berated about prudishness, rigidity, and foolishness. That teenager under siege needs the strong support of friends who say, "You are not alone. Be a clown."

Symptoms of a frightening, nagging disease threaten to cripple a middle-aged man. He grapples with the condition valiantly. Faith and courage are real. Yet some days the fight hardly seems worth it. His patience wears thin. Unperceptive friends ask, "Why don't you just give in to it?" and then say, "Everyone will understand if you go to bed." Such a sufferer can benefit from supportive camaraderie and strengthening counsel: "We understand. Don't give up."

Death has come to a beloved member of a family. For those who are left, life everlasting is now affirmed, not as a theological proposition, but as a profound personal conviction. But visiting doubters spread their philosophy: "Brace up, she's gone. That is all there is." Voices of another perspective must not be muffled: "Hang in there. Grief spawned by death is normal where love is present.

You can go on with reflection and anticipation. There *is* life after life. Your belief is reality, not fantasy."

Tucked away in a little government cubicle is a person who believes that it is possible to be political without succumbing to evil, that civil institutions can serve people, rather than just rule people. This man is trying hard to be a proponent for good and make a substantive contribution to society. Associates frequently laugh at him and label his thoughts and efforts as hopeless idealism. Others are quick to call him a clown. This public servant should receive support: "Your intentions are noble. Your goals are appreciated. Certainly politics can be a highly moral activity. Keep up the good work."

Divorce has almost destroyed a woman's self-confidence. But she continues to believe in the possibility of a durable, loving relationship. Acquaintances discourage and deride her: "Don't be silly. Men can't be trusted. Just live for yourself." But this woman longs for positive sentiments and compassionate comments: "Fresh starts are possible. You can experience true love. If it is silly to believe that, so be it."

Clowns need encouragement.

Clownish Fellowship

Enter the church. Quite possibly no institution is more important to clowns than the church of Jesus Christ. By means of its fellowship, witness, worship, and works, the church encourages clowns.

At the very inception of the church, the membership of the church was suspect. Clamoring to assume leadership in that primitive fellowship were people who had deserted Jesus in his most critical hour; Jesus had entrusted a bold worldwide mission to men who were at first too scared to leave a locked room in Jerusalem. The astounding news of the resurrection of Jesus had to be delivered to his disciples, rather than discovered by them. (And women, society's second-class citizens, to whom few would pay attention, were the bearers of that announcement.) Just imagine, charged as messengers of the gospel were people besieged by questions, doubts, and guilt. Even at the ascension of Jesus these disciples displayed an amazing lack of comprehension regarding the true nature of Christ's Kingdom.

An ancient legend says that after the ascension—when Jesus had returned to heaven as the exalted Christ—some of the angels, archangels, and members of the heavenly host questioned him about his accomplishments on Earth. These inquisitors were astounded both by the small number of his truly dedicated followers and by the very ordinary, even, at times, untrustworthy, nature of these people. The heavenly beings asked Jesus if he was sure that he wanted this group to carry on his work. When Jesus responded affirmatively, his questioners then asked about his alternate plan. They assumed that Jesus had a back-up program. Jesus replied, "I have no other. This group is the only one that I am depending upon, because this group is my church."[1]

The situation did not improve with the passing of time. Paul addressed the constituents of the church in Corinth as saints. Saints! Those people?

The Apostle was writing about people who were divided in their loyalties, immature in their spirituality, argumentative in their opinions, audacious with their gifts, and insensitive to each other's needs. Saints? These uneducated, prejudiced folks were often called fools.

Persecution sharpened self-identification. Incredibly, in the minds of many, followers of Jesus were willing to take on the government of Rome. Even at the risk of losing their limbs, if not their very lives, Christian believers would not utter the words "Caesar is lord." They were adamant in their statement "Jesus is Lord!" How could a simple, pragmatic confession hurt anything? Clowns!

Those Christians who fled to the catacombs understood the comic absurdity of their situation. On the darkened walls of their dwelling, they etched images of Christ as a clown. Of course as his followers, they knew that they were clowns also. And they knew that the very society that scorned them was to be the object of their ministry. Branded as useless outcasts by many, these early Christians were charged to live as agents of redemption for all. Both their claim and their position appeared ludicrous.

But confidence pervaded that underground community. As fools for Christ's sake, they knew they were a part of the foolishness of God, which was, after all, inestimably wiser than the world. At about this time, John, one of the faithful, who had been banished to the Isle of Patmos, wrote a brilliant summary of the community's conviction. The secularists saw it as a joke. But the disciples of Christ were not laughing—rejoicing at the truth of it, yes, but not laughing at it. "The kingdom of this world has become the kingdom of our Lord and of his Christ, and he shall reign for ever and ever" (Rev. 11:15).

A recent author concludes that "the true comic society is the church."[2] Such an opinion is not without significant support. Jesus established "a fool's paradise, a colony of clowns—men and women who dared to live out their dreams, and pay whatever price was asked of them for that privilege."[3]

The church is *a fellowship of love.* By its very nature the church is an inclusive, rather than an exclusive, body. All kinds of people are welcome in this fellowship: rich and poor; sick and healthy; weak and strong; black, brown, yellow, red, and white; economic successes and economic failures; elderly, middle-aged, and young; educated and uneducated; happy and sad. Unity is formed out of terrific diversity. Look at almost any local church, and you probably will discover a most unlikely group of people. Often the only thing that the people hold in common is their relationship to the church.

Perfection is not a prerequisite for association with this fellowship. At one time or another, all within it have failed. Understanding and forgiveness are plentiful. Often the very pillars of the church are people attempting to overcome trouble-packed pasts, people recovering from horrendous hurts, people rebounding from lives in emotional pits.

Though the church exists for mission, its fellowship is as concerned with people as with purpose. Being present for each other is a high priority. Fellow believers are challenged to share one another's burdens as well as blessings, joys as well as sorrows. Church members know both how to laugh and how to cry together.

What a welcome sanctuary for clowns! Hurt because of a lack of appreciation is met with expressions of genuine gratitude. Ridicule because of lofty ideals is replaced with a reminder of what is ultimately real. Rejection provoked by the practice of a boundless breadth of compassion is replaced by a ringing affirmation. Come on, all you clowns: here is where you belong.

The church is *a fellowship of weakness.* At no time has the church ever appeared to be equal to its task. Shadowed by the impressive structures of society, believers always seem to be too poor, too powerless, and too few to make a significant difference for good. Clowns are thoroughly familiar with such negative odds.

The apparent weakness of the church is not to be despised. Take note of the divine design in the Lord's words to the Apostle Paul: "My power is made perfect in weakness" (2 Cor. 12:9). God has done with the world's perception of weakness precisely what he has done with the world's perception of foolishness. In fact, the two are integrally linked. Weakness is as strength and foolishness is as wisdom. Read Paul's startling statement: "The foolishness of God is wiser than men, and the weakness of God is stronger than men" (1 Cor. 1:25). Once again the Apostle from Tarsus is writing autobiography as well as theology. Consider his confession: "For the sake of Christ, then, I am content with weaknesses . . . for when I am weak, then I am strong" (2 Cor. 12:10).

Frequently high priorities for members of the church are objects of scorn for patrons of society. Virtues such as humility and meekness are considered liabilities. For people who place a high value on self-assertion, personal achievement, and private gain, a life devoted to service appears to be a misdirection of energies. Goodness looks for all the world like weakness.

In a fine novel entitled *The Final Beast,* an important point about power and weakness is aptly made. A much maligned minister by the name of Theodore Nicolet—a classic clown—stands before his congregation to preach. The week has been a harrowing one. Nicolet has succumbed to strong temptations. He has been made the brunt of gossipy conversations. His message for this morning, born in great pain, must be delivered from a position of profound weakness. Yet Nicolet's words are gospel—powerful gospel. He says, "Don't believe I preach the best without knowing the worst . . . but the worst isn't the last thing. The last thing is the best. It's the power from on high that comes down into the world that wells up from the rock-bottom worst of the world like a hidden spring. Can you believe it? The last best thing is the laughing. [Do you see that—the laughing?] Deep in the hearts of the saints, sometimes our hearts even. Yes, you are terribly loved and forgiven. Yes, you are healed. All is well."[4]

All is well! Clowns, take heart.

The church is *a fellowship of the spirit.* According to the respected theologian Hans Küng, the church owes its origin, existence, and continued life to the Spirit of God. Küng says, "The church is vivified, sustained, and guided by this spirit, the power and strength of God."[5] Similarly, Jürgen Moltmann writes that the powers of the Spirit are the powers of the church's life.[6] Under the guidance of the Spirit, the church seeks to fulfill the meaning of the ministry of Christ. Think what that means from the point of view that posits Jesus as a clown par excellence.

The history of the Christian church cannot be understood apart from the ministry of the Holy Spirit. Read the inspiring account of the work of the early church in the

New Testament Book of Acts. From the Spirit came the vision that gave the church direction. Major hindrances to the spread of the gospel—such as personal prejudices and social barriers—were overcome by the power of the Spirit. The various gifts and offices needed for effective ministry by the church were provided by the Spirit.

Within a fellowship of the Spirit, dreams are discovered, fundamental convictions are nutured, inspiration for service is received, and skills for action are formed. Such a fellowship welcomes harassed, fatigued, and disillusioned advocates of good will. Does that not bring to mind parade-weary, performance-exhausted clowns who have been hassled because of their actions, taken advantage of because of their good nature, and buffeted about as buffoons?

The church is a fellowship in which noble motives are rekindled, personal strength is renewed, and moral courage is reinforced. In fact the enumeration of the gifts of the Spirit as recorded by Paul reads like an elaboration of the characteristics of clowns: "love, joy, peace, patience, kindness, goodness, faithfulness, gentleness, self-control." (Gal. 5:22–23).

Certainly clowning is a legacy of the church. Good reason exists to believe that clowning may also be a key to the future integrity of the church. The world may never again take the church seriously unless its members become once more fools for Christ. The church welcomes clowns. The church encourages clowns.

Comic Witness

In the holy fool tradition of the Greek and Russian Orthodox churches, the monks periodically assume the garb and the role of a fool. Religious leaders look like and behave like clownish figures. The purpose of this ecclesiastical play is to awaken piety, to encourage a responsible morality, among believers.[7] As Frederick Buechner says, "If the truth is worth telling, it is worth making a fool of yourself to tell."[8]

Now it is one thing to don a fool's cap ritually and to affirm the communicative value of foolishness theoretically, but it is quite another matter to come off looking clownish, looking foolish, when behaving naturally. Yet this is the consequence of taking seriously the comic witness of the church.

At no time has this truth been clearer to me than in a worship service in a church in another city one Sunday morning. I had traveled there for the dual purposes of keeping a speaking engagement and visiting with a critically ill friend. My friend was pastor of the church. He was in the last stages of cancer and thus in the final days of his public ministry.

At the appointed moment in the service, my friend hobbled to the pulpit and with great conviction declared the goodness of God. I could hardly believe what I heard. I could have understood a message about the meaning of pain, the experience of suffering. But the goodness of God? I wrote on the top of my order of service, "How can a man stunned by an inoperable tumor on the brain blare out a word about the goodness of God? What a clown!"

All of the holy fools—those in comical clothes, those in clerical robes, and those in business suits; those with artful masks drawn with greasepaint and those with painful or cheerful looks reflective of personal experience—properly belong in the church. As I noted in chapter 3, inevitably the gospel shapes such persons. And the witness of the church encourages people like that.

Consider *the message of the church.* Floyd Shaffer spells out the interesting relationship that exists between the word *clod*—an Anglo-Saxon term from which the word *clown* was derived—and *doulos,* or "servant"—an ancient Greek word that was a favorite term of Jesus for describing his followers. A clod is the lowest member of the community, an oaf, the one put upon, the person assigned to do the work that no one else will do. Similarly, a *doulos* is a slave, the lowest of the low, a person who does the work that no one else will do.[9]

So strong is the association between *clod* ("clown") and *doulos* ("servant") in Shaffer's mind that he inserts the word *clown* in biblical passages where Jesus uses the word *servant.* Notice the results: "He who is greatest among you shall be your *clown*" Matt. 23:11). "If anyone would be first, he must be last of all and *clown* of all" (Mark 9:35b). "Whoever would be great among you must be your *clown*" (Mark 10:43b).[10] How interesting! What incredible words of encouragement for clowns! And they are holy words.

The message of the church affirms clowns. Within the church, giving is considered more important than receiving, sensitivity and vulnerability are applauded as strengths rather than derided as weaknesses, spontaneity and flexibility are exalted as virtues instead of castigated as vices. Praise exists for the kind of "wise men" who will passionately follow a star. Enthusiastic approval is given to those who cannot contain their joy. A freedom to be unique, different from the rest of society, is provided for each person. People are urged to accept major challenges and to pursue personal dreams. A premium is placed on festivity.

In a series of lessons taken from his Sermon on the Mount, Jesus succinctly summarized the comic witness of the Christian community. Each of his statements was introduced with the word *blessed* or *happy*. That which Jesus praised is that which a clown practices. Read the Lord's words and right away you will see this pertinent truth. "Blessed are you poor, for yours is the kingdom of God" (Luke 6:20). The importance of life cannot be measured by an accumulation of things.

Jesus continued and pronounced as blessed those who ravenously pursued righteousness like a hungry man sought bread or a thirsty woman looked for a drink. How does that sound in a culture preoccupied with the pursuit of success—at any cost? Then there was the matter of mercy. People should not get what they "deserved." Grace—the kind of boundless grace with which God relates to his creation—should prevail in interpersonal relationships. Purity was cherished. Peacemaking was praised. Think of that. Support for peace is not indicative of a suspect patriotism or a Milquetoast disposition. Those who wage peace as aggressively as others wage war are blessed by God.

Jesus knew that people who took him seriously and lived out his teachings faithfully would meet verbal criticism, social ostracism, and perhaps even physical persecution. For this reason he closed this particular message with a promise that the blessings of God would prevail over the negative reactions of society. What more could a clown want to hear!

Though joy is the dominant mood of the church's

message and "Rejoice" its first and last audible word, this joy is not unrealistic, detached, or irrelevant. Christians are not blind to injustice and suffering. Happiness persists because of a conviction that in the light of divine sovereignty, injustice and suffering are not ultimate.[11] As a result of the message of Christ, Christians possess an internal joy that transcends external circumstances. In reviewing both his positive and his negative experiences, and considering times of plenty and occasions of hunger, the Apostle Paul said, "I have learned, in whatever state I am, to be content" (Phil. 4:11).

Consider *the messengers of the church.* If associations with like-minded persons are therapeutic for the soul and energizing for the will, clowns ought to be at their very best when in contact with the church. Here are people resolved to incarnate the message, "the good news," of the church, and committed to living as fools for Christ. When the noted author Malcolm Muggeridge expresses his feelings about joining a local church, he could be describing the sentiments of a clown who finds such a fellowship. Muggeridge speaks of a "sense of homecoming . . . of responding to a bell that has long been ringing."[12]

Prolific in the church are people who have made themselves vulnerable to the world and have been battered. Present as well are people who have expended the last ounces of their energies seeking to sing a song, to provoke a smile, or to deliver the gospel. Debate surrounds people who, in the face of overwhelming odds, stood their ground in favor of a good cause. Some say they eventually lost. But the persons involved insist that they won. Clowns! In their opinion, fidelity is victory.

Preachers are quintessential clowns. All week long they listen to stories of conflict, visit rooms of suffering, and comfort people who are dying. On Sunday they stand behind a pulpit to speak of peace, comfort, and life. They too have sinned: an angry fuss with the family just before leaving home for the service, a blatant lie told, with an elaborate rationale vigorously defended, an adulterous thought buried in the psyche or an adulterous act in the actual past. But listen. Preachers speak of happiness, truth, and fidelity. Forgiveness as a theme for the sermon grows out of forgiveness as the need of the sermonizer.

Sunday after Sunday preachers rise before their congregations to share a word of good news amid all of the bad news, to announce the promise that "you can make it" when plagued by the sickening realization that they may not be "making it." Indeed, "we have this treasure in earthen vessels, to show that the transcendent power belongs to God and not to us" (2 Cor. 4:7).

A few years ago—Easter Sunday evening on the 1982 Eastern Orthodox calendar, to be exact—I was in Arad, Romania, to preach. When I arrived at the site of the service I was overwhelmed. People lined the walkways and stood on the grounds. Entrance into the building was nearly impossible because of the press of the crowd, which, I was told, had started gathering in the middle of Sunday afternoon.

When I finally stepped through the doorway that led to a small platform in that church's sanctuary, I was confronted by a sight that I never will forget: a mass of people. No distinction could be made between seats and aisles. People were everywhere. As I looked more closely,

I realized that a few people were seated in pews. All of the others were standing in every available space or sitting in the windows, on the platform or in the baptistery. In a building intended to hold 1,200 people, 3,000 had gathered.

These believers could meet together only when a government office approved their assembly. Many of them had undergone the harassment of a lengthy interrogation by civil authorities because of their religious faith. Some of them had been severely deprived economically as a result of their persistent spiritual witness. Present that evening to take note of those in attendance at the service and to observe the proceedings for future reference were officials from the Office of the Ministry of Cults, the government watchdog for all religious activities. Here, under critical supervision and the threat of persecution, was a congregation of poor, powerless people.

Many thoughts raced through my mind. I wanted to simply greet these folks in Christ's name, retell the story of the resurrection, and encourage the believers in their pilgrimages. Just seconds before I stood up to preach, my young interpreter stunned me as he whispered, "Don't be easy on them. Preach the gospel."

Don't be easy on them? These folks had taken a risk even to be present. Already their lives were difficult, at best. Faith was tested every day. I thought seriously about the young man's recommendation. Then I realized the point. My interpreter thoroughly understood the gospel and the true nature of its messengers. These people could not give up. Sure, they might look like fools—clowns. All the odds were against them. The smiles on their faces were not created by conducive circumstances. They could speak of hope and influence only out of lives with no status. They would look like clowns. But that was their calling, and they needed to be reminded of it. They still could dream. They still could live with integrity. Oh yes, and they still could express their faith musically. And they did!

In retrospect my dominant impression of that evening in Arad is not one of political oppression or of a repression of religious liberty, but musical expression. I remember most the "hallelujahs"—the hallelujahs! In such an adverse setting, only clowns could have carried the pitch and sung the words. Hallelujah! How true to the identity of authentic messengers of the church were those Romanian Christians. Any clowns would have been proud of that association, strengthened by that congregation.

Why do the message and the messengers of the church—the comic witness of the church—offer so much encouragement to clowns? Conrad Hyers answers: "Human existence . . . as it is religiously lived and understood, is only given adequate definition in terms of a dialectical interplay between seriousness and laughter, between 'holiness' and humor."[13]

The issue of laughter *is* an issue of religious experience. The comic witness of the church offsets the tragic witness of the world, which stifles freedom, producing dogmatism and fanaticism. People who listen to the message of the church are told to be different, to remain open, and to reject rigidity. In reality the comic witness of the church coincides with and reinforces the contribution of a clown showing "us that our pompousness, our yearning after results, our cynicisms are the weapons with which we try to maintain ourselves, weapons which lead to an inauthentic way of living our lives that alienate us from ourselves, from our fellowmen and from the deepest realities of love and hope."[14] No doubt about it, the church encourages clowns.

Festive Worship

For many years the introduction of the pastoral homily for Easter Sunday morning included a joke or a funny story. Having read aloud the biblical narratives about the resurrection, the worship leader would jest with members of the congregation. People laughed, laughed boisterously. A collection of Easter jokes developed. Early church leaders believed that a humorous story was appropriate at the begining of an Easter sermon because laughter is a Christian response to all of life's harshest realities. Life is comedy, not tragedy. Resurrection is a hilarious surprise. Easter Sunday is a day for laughing.

Just as festive days mark the calendar of the church, a festive spirit characterizes the worship of God. Divine invitations to worship spell out the proper intentions and set the course for acceptable actions among worshipers. Chronicler, psalmist and prophet agree on the priority of a human response to God's requirement for worship and praise.

Ascribe to the Lord the glory due his name;
bring an offering and come before him!
Worship the Lord in holy array (1 Chron. 16:29).

O come, let us worship and bow down,
let us kneel before the Lord, our Maker! (Ps. 95:6).

All flesh shall come to worship before me,
says the Lord (Isa. 66:23).

Jesus recognized the expectation of his heavenly Father regarding worship and encouraged his followers to be obedient to it. Later the elderly Apostle named John acclaimed on Patmos what earlier the patriarch Moses had understood on Sinai: "Worship God" (Rev. 22:9).

Nature of worship

Corporate worship has only one purpose: to give glory to God. That purpose determines the approach that is appropriate for participants in worship. In the middle of holy history—within a context of clowning—worshipers gather with a living hope, a vibrant memory, and a joyful spirit. God's redemptive actions are recalled. The holy summons to live as fools is celebrated. Fulfillment of divine promises is anticipated. The dominant mood of such worship is doxology. The most important actions are adoration and praise. A word frequently spoken is "hallelujah," an exuberant exclamation of ecstatic joy.

Old Testament descriptions of worship are dominated by praise. Prevalent in these experiences was a joyful mood, like the mood at the coronation of a king, the arrival of spring, or the celebration of a marriage. In response to the admonition "Let the faithful exult in glory" (Ps. 149:5), praise practically exploded among the people. Individual worshipers sensed that they were a part of a cosmic congregation involving angels, the sun, the moon, stars, the heavens, the waters, sea monsters, beasts, cattle, creeping things, and birds (Ps. 148). Human voices declaring praise to God were joined by the triumphant and happy sounds of trumpets, lutes, harps, timbrels, strings, pipes, and loudly clashing cymbals. (Ps. 150:3–6). Participants in worship sang and danced, played and prayed. No doubt some spectators surmised that the worshipers were making fools of themselves.

Jesus was a loyal patron of this tradition of worship. Not only did he participate faithfully in the services of the local synagogue, he went regularly to the major festivals in Jerusalem. Both in his words and his deeds Jesus embraced the festive spirit of worship.

Even extravagance was praised. On one occasion in Bethany, Jesus gladly accepted a spontaneous, costly display of devotion from a woman with a questionable reputation. When some of his disciples criticized the action as wasteful and castigated the woman as irresponsible, Jesus stopped their talk and offered his opinion: "She has done a beautiful thing" (Mark 14:6). While in the temple in Jerusalem, Jesus observed the offering of a poor widow. As an act of divine worship, the woman placed in the temple treasury two small coins—all that she had. Jesus praised her profusely.

Jesus spoke of the end time in terms of a banquet. Life and worship in the presence of God were likened to participating in an eternal feast: the messianic banquet. All of the happy associations commonly made with a festive occasion were appropriate. This experience of high worship would involve talking and laughing, fellowship and joy.

Another example of Jesus' attitude toward festivity and worship occurred as Jesus entered Jerusalem for his final Passover there. Actually the scene was rather comic. Have you ever seen a grown man bouncing along on the back of a short-legged little donkey? Many times when traveling in the Middle East that very sight has brought a smile to my face. I have been reminded of an oversized clown straddling an undersized motorcycle. But Jesus' arrival in Jerusalem marked a serious moment. The King was entering the holy city.

Multitudes lined the rough road that wound its way into Jerusalem. As Jesus and his meager, motley entourage of followers—men and women—approached, the crowds sensed a messianic event. Some of the onlookers gathered palm leaves and threw them in the path of the prophet from Nazareth. Others laid their garments in his way. Children ran and shouted playfully. Adults called out holy words confessionally: "Hosanna!" "Blessed is he who comes in the name of the Lord!" Apparently Jesus welcomed such hilarity. In fact, he remarked to some of his critics that if the human voices were silenced, even the stones would cry out. Any clown would have been buoyed by the festive spirit of those worshipers who watched this parade.

The Apostle Paul provides us with insights into the worship practices of the early churches. Worshipers joyfully lifted their voices in the singing of psalms, hymns, and spiritual songs (Eph. 5:19, Col. 3:16). Scriptures were read and interpreted. Members of the congregations interacted with worship leaders, speaking aloud such spiritually significant words as *maranatha* (our Lord come) "Abba" (father), and "amen" (truly or so be it). Most often communion was shared in thanksgiving. A spirit of celebration prevailed.

A pinnacle of festive worship was reached in the memorable vision of heaven recorded in the Book of Revelation. A cosmic congregation was assembled: creatures of the Earth, elders of the church, and myriads of angels. The air was filled with shouting and singing as worshipers rejoiced, exulted, and gave glory to God. Spirit-lifting, heartwarming litanies were affirmed by all:

"Hallelujah! Salvation and glory and power belong to our God" (Rev. 19:1), "Worthy is the Lamb" (Rev. 5:12). "Honor and glory and blessing" (Rev. 4:12), "Hallelujah! For the Lord our God the Almighty reigns" (Rev. 19:6).

Not all such worship is confined to the biblical past or projected only as a future hope. One year on the first Sunday evening of Advent, near the conclusion of a communal singing of Handel's *Messiah,* my attention was captivated by the actions of a little girl. She was seated at the very front of the sanctuary. The "Hallelujah Chorus" was under way. This little girl was completely committed to the spirit of the moment. She gave herself to it without reservation, oblivious to all about her—to the sound of the symphony orchestra, to the harmony of the choir, to the unified voice of the congregation.

As I looked more closely and listened carefully. I realized she was shouting, "Hallelujah"—off key but with emotion, without any contribution to the melody but as a living lesson in authenticity. Here was a true act of worship. The little woman just stood there shouting, "Hallelujah"—unconcerned about the opinions of her peers and not worried about the sound of her voice. She was responding to one glorious moment in worship, as all people are to respond to every moment in worship. Hallelujah!

Gaiety, spontaneity, and freedom—each a high priority for clowns—are basic characteristics of authentic communal worship. Festivity so dominates the communal worship of God that Jesus likened it to a party. Think of that. A call to worship is an invitation to a party. And everyone knows how much clowns love a party.

Sometimes the very nature of a specific service of worship is especially conducive to clownish behavior.

Imagine thinking that getting wet in a baptistery has something to do with a quality of discipleship and a life of integrity. Study a lone person kneeling at an altar rail praying about events that affect the whole Earth. What is the significance of her family simply lighting candles in a wreath to participate in the long wait of Advent? What could possibly be the relationship between an action such as that and anticipation of the coming of Christ or the salvation of the world?

Late on a winter Wednesday afternoon, observe adults dressed in business suits and fashionable dresses going about their tasks with ashes smeared on their foreheads in the sign of a cross. Then reflect on an entire congregation sitting in silent darkness awaiting the Easter dawn and believing that the promise of that situation has something to do with the redcemption of all creation. Watch worshipers moved to tears of joy merely by munching on some bits of unleavened bread and drinking hardly a full swallow of grape juice. Clowns!

Benefits of worship

Though the purpose of worship is to praise God, worship benefits believers—individually and as a group. All of the Christian life is enriched. Faith, hope, and love are strengthened. Mission and ministry are enhanced. Perhaps a German mystic explains it best with his observation that "What we become in the presence of God, that we can be all day long."[15] Conversely, apart from regular experiences of worship, ministers lose their strength for ministering, choirs cease to find joy in singing, and clowns forget why they are clowning.

Festive worship nurtures the presence of wonder: an appreciation for the transcendent in our midst and a sense of mystery, apart from which real religion does not exist. As wonder develops, the common earth becomes holy ground. Nothing is taken for granted. A happy appreciation exists for the roar of an ocean, the scent of a rose, the uniqueness of a four-leaf clover, the glory of a sunset, and the quiet of a snowfall.

Even more important, with the emergence of wonder come the understanding of the possibility of surprise and the availability of hope. People realize that life is not predictable—at any moment it can change for the better. Wonder frees people from making decisions by cold calculations and frees people for making relations that defy rationalization. Faith develops more as poetry than as science. The capacity for wonder is accompanied by a sensitivity to the rhythms of creation and to those events that only can be described as miracles—facilitators of a new creation.

Similarly, festive worship gives birth to a confident joy. In fact, Sam Shoemaker says, "The surest mark of a Christian is not faith, or even love, but joy."[16] Christians are eucharistic people: always rejoicing, always giving thanks. Oh, sure, tears and the situations that cause them still come. But laughter is more basic—deeper than tears. No situation is ultimately threatening. Promise prevails. Little wonder that Paul from Tarsus could taunt even the sinister specter of death.

This truth of confident joy—so celebrated in worship—was powerfully driven into my consciousness during an extended period of sadness and need. The medium was a message from my good friend Grady Nutt, whose untimely death continued to cause hurt. One morning the mail brought a brief note from Eleanor Nutt and these words from her late husband: "When the world shakes its

fist and says, Good Friday! God comes back with dog-
wood, redbuds, and jonquils; with the crocuses and
butterflies of life and says, Easter! Easter! Easter!"

Festive worship stirs enthusiasm as it creates a buoyant
spirit. Spiritlessness—the deadly enemy of true religion—is replaced by abundant life. Born in worship is an
irrepressible vigor—a zest—for all that is good. Words
that John Killinger wrote about preaching apply equally
well to worship: "In the end, it is the miracle of [worship,]
the magic of the gospel, that dispels the gloom again from
this much-miracled, time-wearied Camelot of ours, and
sets its knights and ladies all adance again. Nothing else
can out-Merlyn it; it is the supreme gift of God to this
soul-spent, jag-jaded age we live in."[17]

Remember the party analogy. This is how Robert
Farrar Capon perceives worship as he describes its impact
on participants. Capon advises, "You go to taste and see
how gracious the inveterately hospitable Lord is. To share
still another bottle of the great old wine he has always
kept your cellar full of. And to relish once again the old
tall tale about how he came to his own party in disguise
and served the devil a rubber duck. You go in short to
have a ball—to keep company while you roll over your
tongue the delectable things which have been yours all
along but which get better every time you taste them."[18]

Consequences of worship

A worshipful look toward God results in an ethical life
in the world. To see God clearly and to worship God
festively is to gain insight into the needs of neighbors and
to discover the power for ministry. In no sense is worship
an escape from moral problems or a retreat from social
service. John A. T. Robinson labels as "the essence of

religious perversion" that worship which is a withdrawal from the world "to be with God—even if it is only in order to receive strength to go back into it."[19] William H. Willimon agrees and argues that "the sincerity of our thankfulness in worship will be judged by whether or not we show forth that thankfulness in our self-giving to others."[20] What is done in a person's worship is to be embraced in that person's ethics until all of life "is one continuous act of eucharistia."[21]

Every single act of worship contains ethical implications for life in the world. For example, gratitude to God for his gifts to us precipitates a gracious sharing of our personal gifts with others. Prayer—"defined in terms of penetration through the world to God"[22]—is "the responsibility to meet others with all I have."[23] Offering is a costly commitment "to become the good work of God in the world."[24] Communion—participation in the Lord's Supper—gives rise to a conviction about the necessity of sharing bread with all who hunger.

Because of their awareness of the integral relationship between festive worship and effective service, civil rights movement activists regularly met for worship in churches before and after their work on the streets. Celebrations of worship have sparked initiatives for peace, efforts at community reconciliation, attempts to facilitate justice by offering legal aid, and agitation for responsible environmental regulations. Christian worship suggests, supports, and strengthens—indeed, encourages—the kinds of activities that keep clowns busy.

Hilarious Ministry

Christianity and ministry are inseparable. An affirmation of ministry is the heart of every celebration of the gospel. Ministers of Christ—"up-and-coming dabblers in the down-and-out"[25]—constitute the membership of the church: a community of clowns. Those who view the ministry of Christ as ridiculous inevitably consider the ministry of Christ's church to be hilarious.

To fully grasp the importance of ministry in all of its hilarity, study the biblical definition of true religion and ponder the personal example of Jesus. In the brief New Testament epistle that bears the name of James, true religion is equated with—get this—taking care of widows and orphans while keeping yourself from being corrupted by the world (James 1:27). Charity and purity! Can you imagine so mundane a matter as the care of the unfortunate taking on eternal importance?

Actually such an understanding of authentic religion is very similar to the Old Testament view epitomized by Micah. This ancient prophet raises the question of what is good and "what does the Lord require of you." He records the answer: "To do justice, to love kindness [or to practice steadfast love] and to walk humbly with your God" (Micah 6:8). In both instances devotion to God finds its most fundamental expression in a ministry to people, especially the dispossessed.

Jesus affirmed the centrality of ministry both in his teachings and his actions. At the conclusion of one particularly popular parable affirming ministry, Jesus defined a widespread application of its major truth. He told how a traveler had discovered a man in a ditch and—foolishly, according to conventional wisdom—bound his wounds and provided for his extended care. Then Jesus said to all who heard or read his words, "Go and do likewise" (Luke 10:37)—an indisputable commission to behave as fools on behalf of compassionate ministry.

In a most memorable parable on the final judgment, Jesus established ministry to persons in need as the solitary criterion upon which life in the Kingdom of God was granted. Astoundingly absent from his remarks were references to creedal confessions or conformity with orthodoxy. Pervasively present was an indication of the eternal importance of ministry. Jesus held up as kingdom events the kind of commonplace activities—seemingly insignificant deeds—of which any clown is capable: sharing a cup of water or a piece of bread, welcoming a stranger, visiting a prisoner, caring for one who is ill, and distributing clothes to the ill clad. Christ taught that he so closely identified with the needy and hurting members of society that ministry to them was ministry to him. The very kinds of activities that many people consider worthless or a waste of time and label as a comic enterprise or a laughable involvement are the ministries that Jesus commended and blessed.

Had there been any lingering doubt about the disposition of Jesus regarding ministry, that would have been settled completely on the Thursday evening prior to his crucifixion. Contrary to cultural tradition, as well as to popular messianic expectation, Jesus took a towel and kneeled before his disciples to wash their feet. Not surprisingly, these men were nervous and uncomfortable with this gesture. In fact, if the scene had not been so serious, it would have been funny: the very idea of the mighty Messiah in such a position of vulnerability and humility. You know the loud-mouthed consensus of a success-oriented culture—who but a fool would identify superiority with humility, security with vulnerability, strength with weakness, and greatness with service?

A second-century manual on church discipline states

that if a person is willing to share what lasts forever, that person should be even more willing to share things that do not last. That is the way of a follower of Christ. The way of a clown! With care a Christian embraces those with inadequate food, insufficient housing, incomplete education, and acts to meet their needs. Patiently and compassionately the Christian moves to reduce suffering, to heal hurts, and to bind up brokenness. From a laughably precarious but religiously precious posture of care, guilt is confronted with grace, sin with forgiveness, doubt with conviction, despair with hope, and anxiety with peace. Perhaps a commission to such ministry should include the provision of a foolscap.

So it goes in the life of the church. Ministries often provoke mockery. Ministers frequently look like clowns. See an enthusiastic young missionary in some remote region, convinced that a word fitly spoken can lead an entire community to redemption. Observe a counselor whose service to her clients consists of concerned listening. Can listening be considered a ministry that helps resolve problems? Watch a uniformed member of the Salvation Army standing at the entrance to a shopping mall, tending a little black kettle for coins, ringing a bell, cheerfully mouthing Christmas greetings and inviting contributions, firmly believing that eventually this action will help hurting people and glorify God.

When Henri M. Nouwen visited Rome, he was most impressed by the clowns he met: students tutoring grade school dropouts and the elderly; a nun spending all of her energy assisting two helpless, home-bound women; young people helping drunks to get off the street and find food; a priest working to establish community among handicapped people.[26]

Actually the whole world is full of such clowning: I know a small group of middle-aged women and men who regularly visit the residents of a nursing home for the elderly, knowing that many of the patients will not even remember their kindness, and a committee of four who opened a downtown shelter for the homeless as one small response to a major social problem. Then there is a conscientious retiree who daily devotes time to stocking a food closet to provide for the undernourished citizens of the city, and a high school student who patiently tutors an elementary school child from a deprived family. And among the other clowns I know are college classmates working to restore a house in a deteriorating neighborhood, a doctor devoting a portion of his work day to a cost-free program of rehabilitation for drug addicts, and a businessperson establishing a job training school as her positive response to the specter of poverty. Clowns abound. Observe them everywhere selflessly attacking unnecessary suffering and instilling hope.

A story has it that one day the wife of the founder of the Salvation Army was found in a ditch caring for a drunkard. Her nice clothing was covered with the intoxicated man's excrement. A passerby noticed the sight and commented to the woman, "I would not do that for a million dollars." The woman responded, "I would not either!" Such are the cost and commitment of ministry—yes, hilarious ministry.

Paul's startling judgment from the past still stands. Divinely inspired action is unintelligible to human reason. God's foolishness is wiser than human wisdom. Look back. Only through the folly of humiliation was Jesus able to offer salvation. Critics called the Savior a clown.

Look around. In a world of schisms, divisions, rivalries,

and conflicts, only a dangerous as well as foolish act of reconciliation can establish communion among people and develop community for people. Society is enriched and people are helped by simple services that often appear insignificant and unsuccessful. The weak receive more attention than the strong. Faithfulness rather than success is the primary measure of ministry.

Note the response of Jesus to people involved in acts of hilarious ministry. In Matthew 25 Jesus reserves the word "blessed" for these very people. "Blessed!" Strike up the band, release the balloons, string up the confetti, whistle with all your might. These are activities appropriate to the spirit of this word: "Blessed!" Here is the ultimate judgment, the final affirmation, the only comment that really matters, regarding ministry and those who minister. Jesus says to ministers as a group, "Blessed" (Matt. 25:34) and to each minister individually, "Well done, good and faithful servant" (Matt. 25:21, 23). Today the church—the body of Christ in the world—conveys those sentiments of its Lord. The church encourages clowns.

An old Hasidic parable relates how one of the Just Men came to Sodom to save its people from sin. Night and day he walked the streets and visited the marketplaces, preaching against greed, theft, falsehood, and indifference. At first people listened to him attentively and smiled kindly. But the day came when people stopped listening. They were no longer amused by him. Sinners went on sinning. Situations worsened. One day a child approached the Just Man inquisitively: "Poor stranger, you shout, you expend yourself body and soul. Don't you see it is hopeless?' ' The Just Man answered, "Yes, I see." "Then why do you go on?" the child asked. The Just Man said, "I'll tell you why. In the beginning I thought I could change humanity. Today I know I cannot. If I still shout today, if I still scream, it is to prevent humanity from ultimately changing me."

As I read that parable and think of the Just Man's spiritual kin, silent screams well up within my soul: No! Don't quit! Surely there are others. You are not the only clown. Keep at it until we can get reinforcements. The situation is changeable. Then comes the rush of that persistent question, Where are the clowns?

Maybe a clown convention is in order. Certainly clowns could benefit from getting together. The church really should take the responsibility for bringing off this activity. By means of its fellowship, witness, worship, and ministry, the church is a significant force of encouragement for clowns. Within the church clowns can enjoy fellowship with each other, review the pathos of our time, cry awhile, and then laugh quietly. Who knows, perhaps even a festival or some other kind of celebration can occur.

It is true, of course, that some scoffers will deride the clowns. A few people may even want to get rid of them. You can bet that an attempt will be made to have all comic characters put away. That is to be expected. Members of the church understand. Despair is well known because of the dominance of a cross in the disciples' experience. But a sense of victory is also present because of the promise of an empty tomb. Consequently members of the church are good at crying and laughing, sobbing and singing. Provision of a place of ready acceptance for clowns will always be an important part of the life of the church. After all, the best known of all the early Apostles of the church, one who helped to strengthen the church and define its mission, explained the church's openness to clowns by way of his honest assessment of the fellowship of believers: "We are fools for Christ's sake" (1 Cor. 4:10).

Where are the clowns? The church needs to know the answer to that question. Clowns, step forward. Identify yourselves. No one should be left out. The church wants to convene a massive gathering of clowns, wants to host a celebration and offer encouragement.

Epilogue

Where are the clowns? I hope I've not unduly belabored that question for you. Honestly, it is a persistent question for me.

Where *are* the clowns? This much is sure: God has called clowns in the past and still does today. The gospel gives life to clowns and shapes their characters.

The world needs clowns. Oh, how the world needs them! We have to have people among us who are well versed in tragedy and victory, people who can cry and laugh, and people for whom the ideal is real.

Where are the clowns? The church needs to know in order to get the clowns together for the reassurance of encouragement and the strength for community. If you are one of the clowns, terrific! God bless you! Maintain your identity and continue your much-needed ministry of service.

If you want to become one of the clowns, good! Take courage and be of good cheer. The fellowship of clowns is wide open to new members. You are welcome to walk with Christ and among his people.

Where are the clowns? You see, that question has relevance for God, for the gospel, and for the church, as well as for every person. Where are they, then, these fools for Christ's sake? Where are the clowns?

Notes

1. WHERE ARE THE CLOWNS?

1. Frederick Buechner, *The Sacred Journey* (San Francisco: Harper & Row, Publishers, 1982), 9.
2. Gerhard Kittel, ed., *Theological Dictionary of the New Testament*, Geoffrey W. Bromiley, ed. and trans. vol. 4 (Grand Rapids, Mich.: William B. Eerdmans Publishing Company, 1967), 841.
3. Ibid., 846.
4. Wolfgang M. Zucker, "The Clown as the Lord of Disorder," *Theology Today*, 24 (October 1964):313.
5. William Willeford, *The Fool and His Scepter: A Study in Clowns and Jesters and Their Audience* (Evanston, IL: Northwestern University Press, 1969), 12.
6. Ibid., 10.
7. One particularly helpful piece that I found after I had first preached on the subject of clowns was a sermon by a friend. Interestingly, the author, who grew up in an area of Texas in which I later pastored, was also struck by the rich religious symbolism of the rodeo clown. This sermon can be found in Bill J. Leonard, *Word of God Across the Ages* (Nashville: Broadman Press, 1981), 13–18.
8. Harvey Cox, *The Feast of Fools: A Theological Essay on Festivity and Fantasy* (Cambridge, MA: Harvard University Press, 1969), 132.
9. Frederick Buechner, *Telling the Truth: The Gospel as Tragedy, Comedy, and Fairy Tale* (New York: Harper & Row, Publishers, 1977), 68.

2. GOD CALLS THEM

1. Horace M. Kallen, *Liberty, Laughter, and Tears: Reflections on the Relations of Comedy and Tragedy to Human Freedom* (DeKalb, IL: Northern Illinois University Press, 1968), 69.
2. Frederick Buechner, *Telling the Truth: The Gospel as Tragedy, Comedy, and Fairy Tale* (New York: Harper & Row, Publishers, 1977), 58.
3. Samuel H. Miller, "The Clown in Contemporary Art," *Theology Today* 24 (October 1964):319.
4. Colin Morris, *The Hammer of the Lord* (New York: Abingdon Press, 1973), 97.

5. William Willeford, *The Fool and His Scepter: A Study in Clowns and Jesters and Their Audience* (Evanston, IL: Northwestern University Press, 1969), 232.
6. Buechner, *Telling the Truth*, 63.
7. Elton Trueblood, *The Humor of Christ* (New York: Harper & Row, Publishers, 1964), 63.
8. Morris, *The Hammer of the Lord*, 97.
9. Willeford, *The Fool and His Scepter*, 48–49.
10. Frederick Buechner, *A Room Called Remember: Uncollected Pieces* (San Francisco: Harper & Row, Publishers, 1984), 94.
11. Wolfgang M. Zucker, "The Clown as the Lord of Disorder," *Theology Today* 24 (October, 1964):316.

3. THE GOSPEL SHAPES THEM

1. Colin Morris, *The Hammer of the Lord* (New York: Abingdon Press, 1973), 97.
2. Samuel H. Miller, "The Clown in Contemporary Art," *Theology Today* 24 (October 1964):328.
3. Enid Welsford, *The Fool: His Social and Literary History* (Gloucester, MA: Peter Smith, 1966), 321.
4. William Willeford, *The Fool and His Scepter: A Study in Clowns and Jesters and Their Audience* (Evanston, IL: Northwestern University Press, 1969), 70.
5. Heinrich Böll, *The Clown*, trans. Seila Vennewitz (New York: McGraw-Hill Book Company, 1965), 141.
6. Harvey Cox, *The Feast of Fools: A Theological Essay on Festivity and Fantasy* (Cambridge, MA: Harvard University Press, 1959), 142.
7. Wolfgang M. Zucker, "The Clown as the Lord of Disorder," *Theology Today* 24 (October 1964):307.
8. Ibid., 308.
9. Böll, *The Clown*, 179.
10. Hans Küng, *On Being a Christian*, trans. Edward Quinn (Garden City, NY: Doubleday & Co., Inc., 1976), 274.
11. Welsford, *The Fool*, xii.
12. Heije Faber, "Second Thoughts on the Minister as a Clown," *Pastoral Psychology* 28 (Winter 1979):134.
13. Walter Kerr, *Tragedy and Comedy* (New York: Simon and Schuster, 1967), 335.
14. Henri J. M. Nouwen, *Clowning in Rome: Reflections on Solitude, Celibacy, Prayer, and Contemplation* (Garden City, NY: Image Books, 1979), 3.
15. Morris West, *The Clowns of God* (New York: William Morrow and Company, Inc., 1981), 248.

16. Ibid., 272.
17. Robert E. Neale, "The Crucifixion as Play" in Jürgen Moltmann, *The Theology of Play*, trans. Reinhard Ulrich (New York: Harper & Row, Publishers, 1972), 83.

4. THE WORLD NEEDS THEM

1. Heije Faber, "Second Thoughts on the Minister as a Clown," *Pastoral Psychology* 28 (Winter 1979):132.
2. Frederick Patka, *The Clowns* (Albany, NY: Magi Books, 1964), xiii.
3. Eric Auerbach, *Mimesis* (Princeton, NJ: Princeton University Press, 19534), 305, 307–308, cited in Samuel H. Miller, "The Clown in Contemporary Art," *Theology Today* 24 (October 1964):321.
4. Miller, "The Clown in Contemporary Art," 327.
5. Norman Cousins, *Anatomy of an Illness as Perceived by the Patient: Reflections on Healing and Regeneration* (New York: Bantam Books, 1981), 39.
6. Henlee Barnette, *Exploring Medical Ethics* (Macon, GA: Mercer University Press, 1982), 145.
7. Martin E. Marty, *Friendship* (Allen, TX: Argus Communications, 1980), 66.
8. Eugene Kennedy, *On Being a Friend* (New York: Continuum, 1982), 102.
9. Ibid., 97.
10. Leo Buscaglia, *Loving Each Other: The Challenge of Human Relationships* (Thorofare, NJ: Slack, Incorporated, 1984), 146.
11. Emmett Kelly with F. Beverly Kelley, *Clown* (New York: Prentice-Hall, 1954), 97.
12. Ibid., 126.
13. Reinhold Niebuhr, "Humour and Faith," in *Twenty Centuries of Great Preaching: An Encyclopedia of Preaching*, ed. Clyde E. Fant, Jr., and William M. Pinson, Jr., vol. 10 (Waco, TX: Word Books, Publisher, 1971), 373.
14. Kelly, *Clown*, 49.
15. Walter Kerr, *Tragedy and Comedy* (New York: Simon and Schuster, 1967), 16.
16. Ibid., 340.
17. Harvey Cox, *The Feast of Fools: A Theological Essay on Festivity and Fantasy* (Cambridge, MA: Harvard University Press, 1969), 161.
18. Ibid., p. 144.
19. Buscaglia, *Loving Each Other*, 111.
20. Frederick Buechner, *Now and Then* (San Francisco: Harper & Row, Publishers, 1983), 73.
21. Miller, "The Clown in Contemporary Art," 322.

22. Ibid.
23. William Willeford, *The Fool and His Scepter: A Study in Clowns and Jesters and Their Audience* (Evanston, IL: Northwestern University Press, 1969), 4, 8.
24. Morris West, *The Clowns of God* (New York: WIlliam Morrow and Company, Inc., 1981), 219.
25. Heinrich Böll, *The Clown,* trans. Seila Vennewitz (New York: McGraw-Hill Book Company, 1965), 169.
26. Ibid., 240.
27. West, *The Clowns of God,* 255.
28. M. Conrad Hyers, "The Ancient Zen Master as Clown-Figure and Comic Midwife," *Philosophy East and West* 20 (January 1970):7.
29. Buscaglia, *Loving Each Other,* 176.
30. Robert L. Birch, "Wit and the Emancipators," *Vital Speeches of the Day* 47:16 (June 1, 1981):536.
31. Ibid.
32. Howard Thurman, *With Head and Heart: The Autobiography of Howard Thurman* (New York: Harcourt Brace Jovanoviah, 1979), 140.
33. Mother Teresa, *Words To Love by . . .* (Notre Dame, IN: Ave Maria Press, 1983), 31.
34. Malcolm Muggeridge, *Something Beautiful for God: Mother Teresa of Calcutta* (Garden City, NY: Image Books, 1977), 31.
35. Albert Schweitzer, *Out of My Life and Thought: An Autobiography,* trans. C. T. Campion (New York: Mentor Books, 1963), 74.
36. Kelly, *Clown,* 270–71.

5. THE CHURCH ENCOURAGES THEM

1. William D. Watley, *Sermons on Special Days: Preaching Through the Year in the Black Church* (Valley Forge, VA: Judson Press, 1987), 74–75.
2. M. Conrad Hyers, *And God Created Laughter: The Bible as Divine Comedy* (Atlanta: John Knox Press, 1987), 75.
3. Colin Morris, *The Hammer of the Lord* (New York: Abingdon Press, 1973), 94.
4. Frederick Buechner, *The Final Beast* (San Francisco: Harper & Row, Publishers, 1965), 174–75.
5. Hans Küng, *The Church* (Garden City, NY: Image Books, 1976), 228.
6. Jürgen Moltmann, *The Church in the Power of the Spirit* (New York: Harper & Row, Publishers, 1975), 34.
7. M. Conrad Hyers, "The Ancient Zen Master as Clown-Figure and Comic Midwife," *Philosophy East and West* 20 (January 1970):1.
8. Frederick Buechner, *Telling the Truth: The Gospel as Tragedy, Comedy, and Fairy Tale* (New York: Harper & Row, Publishers, 1977), 5.

9. Floyd Shaffer, *If I Were a Clown* (Minneapolis, MN: Augsburg Publishing House, 1984), 78.
10. Ibid., 79.
11. Elton Trueblood, *The Humor of Christ* (New York: Harper & Row, Publishers, 1964), 32.
12. Geoffrey Barlow, ed. *Vintage Muggeridge: Religion and Society,* (Grand Rapids, MI: William B. Eerdmans Publishing Company, 1985), 167.
13. Hyers, "The Ancient Zen Master as Clown Figure and Comic Midwife," 4.
14. Heije Faber, "Second Thoughts on the Minister as a Clown," *Pastoral Psychology* 28 (Winter 1979):134.
15. Raymond Abba, *Principles of Christian Worship* (New York: Oxford University Press, 1966), 13.
16. Donald E. Demoray, *Laughter, Joy, and Healing* (Grand Rapids, MI: Baker Book House, 1986), 48.
17. John Killinger, *The Centrality of Preaching in the Total Task of the Ministry* (Waco, TX: Word Books, Publisher, 1969).
18. Robert Farrar Capon, *Hunting the Divine Fox: An Introduction to the Language of Theology* (San Francisco: Harper & Row, 1986), 155.
19. John A. T. Robinson, *Honest to God* (Philadelphia: The Westminster Press, 1963), 86–87.
20. William H. Willimon, *The Service of God: Christian Work and Worship* (Nashville, TN: Abingdon Press, 1983), 203.
21. Ibid.
22. Robinson, *Honest to God,* 97.
23. Ibid., 100.
24. Willimon, *The Service of God,* 199.
25. Frederick Buechner, *Now and Then* (San Francisco: Harper & Row, Publishers, 1983), 28.
26. Henri J. M. Nouwen, *Clowning in Rome: Reflections on Solitude, Celibacy, Prayer, and Contemplation,* (Garden City, NY: Image Books, 1979), 1–2.